Black Students
at White Colleges

Charles V. Willie
Arline Sakuma McCord

The Praeger Special Studies program—utilizing the most modern and efficient book production techniques and a selective worldwide distribution network—makes available to the academic, government, and business communities significant, timely research in U.S. and international economic, social, and political development.

Black Students
at White Colleges

PRAEGER SPECIAL STUDIES IN U.S. ECONOMIC AND SOCIAL DEVELOPMENT

Praeger Publishers   New York   Washington   London

PRAEGER PUBLISHERS
111 Fourth Avenue, New York, N.Y. 10003, U.S.A.
5, Cromwell Place, London S.W.7, England

Published in the United States of America in 1972
by Praeger Publishers, Inc.

Library of Congress Catalog Card Number: 72-80468

Printed in the United States of America

Dedicated to
Benjamin Elijah Mays,
President Emeritus of Morehouse College,
a black student who endured, transcended, and overcame

Black Students at White Colleges is based on a study conducted on four predominantly white college campuses in upstate New York during the 1969-70 school year. It was financed by a grant from the Ford Foundation, which is acknowledged with appreciation.

The April 1969 events at Cornell University led us to propose this study. Blacks there seized a building because of unresolved grievances and then obtained firearms, allegedly to protect themselves from white students whom they described as hostile and threatening. The events at Cornell demonstrated that all was not well between student blacks and whites—that there was poor communication between the races. We insisted that our study should attempt to uncover from the black student point of view what was troubling them.

The study was launched during a period when it was becoming increasingly difficult to study black populations. Blacks are on guard against being exploited and being used as a source of data for the development of social science theories that do not proffer any particular benefit to them. Blacks have complained vehemently that they usually fail to benefit from such research.

We tried diligently to protect them against this kind of exploitation, first, by appointing student consultants from the four campuses to our research staff and financially compensating them for their advice and help; second, by giving survey respondents a modest payment for the time required to fill out a rather lengthy questionnaire; and third, by going before a representative black student group on three of the four campuses to explain the study and to respectfully ask the group's permission to conduct the investigation. In the sessions where permission was sought to come on campus and conduct the study, we frankly voiced to the black students our opinion that many whites on most college campuses have little understanding of blacks, their problems, and experiences. We indicated that one of the goals of our study was to discover ways of improving the quality of the campus environment and the educational experience for blacks.

We shared with black students our hope that they would look upon the study as a way of telling the public what it is like to be black at a white college. We have, in this design, attempted to follow W. I. Thomas' theorem: It is essential in the study of man to know just how men define the situations in which they find themselves, because "if men define situations as real, they are real in their consequences."* We emphasized that our basic concern was to understand the kinds of adaptations black students make and why they make these adaptations, from their own point of view.

Whites too readily assume that blacks on white college campuses are there to learn how to succeed in a white world. Projections of this kind lead to faulty conclusions that tend to further becloud a complex and confused situation. We attempted to depart from the old approach. This is a study of the adaptations of black students on white college campuses and not necessarily an assessment of their adjustment.

Four different colleges in New York State were studied: (a) a large, private college located in a country metropolitan area with a population of nearly 500,000; (b) a two-year community college in the same area; (c) a four-year state-operated liberal arts college in a small city of 23,000; and (d) a two-year technical school in a rural village. We identified these institutions as Cosmopolitan, Metropolitan, Small City, and Little Village colleges. Colleges in diverse settings and of varying circumstances were chosen to provide a comparative perspective. Names of the colleges and their communities are fictitious to protect the anonymity of individuals and the good will of the institutions.

Data were gathered from interviews with individual black students and from tape-recorded meetings of several small groups of black students. Survey data were collected from a random sample of white and black students on the four campuses.

Basic planning for the study was a team effort undertaken by Charles Willie, Study Director; Arline Sakuma McCord, Assistant Study Director; and John Dopyera, Field Coordinator. It may be of interest to point out that the senior planners of the study are a black, a brown, and a white person. Hopefully, the varying experiences and backgrounds of the researchers have had a self-correcting effect upon team decisions.

---

*W. I. Thomas in Robert K. Merton, Social Structure and Social Theory (New York: The Free Press, 1949), p. 301.

The field interviewers who conducted in-depth conversations with black students throughout the year were black, brown, and white. They met regularly as a group to share their experiences and observations. We are indeed grateful to the interviewers who faced the initial reactions of suspicion, mistrust, and fear but who established a sufficiently secure bond of humanity with the black students to obtain rich and revealing information. Interviewers were Jim Allaway, LaVern Bass, Charles Hicks, Joan Levy, Hurclee (Bill) Maye, Susan Mingolelli, Mercedes Myers, Robert Ybarra, and Sandra Robinson. William Mangin assisted as an interviewer of black college administrators.

Outstanding clerical assistance in transcribing field data and keeping records up-to-date was provided by Jane Bergdorf and Gerry Victor. We are especially grateful to the student secretaries at the Powelson Business Institute for transcribing difficult conference tapes. We also acknowledge with appreciation typing assistance rendered by Mary Belle Isle, Mary Walsh, and Nancy Oshiro.

Joan Levy and Harvey Greisman performed excellently as research assistants in preparing the data for analysis. Gene Wittkopf and Carlton Hornung were good technical consultants, who assisted in processing the survey data through the computer. We are grateful to James Gies and Dorothy Sickels for their fine copy editing work. Finally, the study could not have been launched or concluded without the cooperation of the black advisors on the four college campuses and the black student consultants whose names we cannot reveal without revealing the institutions with which they are affiliated. Such a revelation would be contrary to our initial agreement with the administrators and students of these colleges.

To the black students at white colleges we give our thanks and confess our admiration. We appreciate the way they took us into their confidence. We hope that the following pages will faithfully tell their story and that it will be read with care, compassion, and understanding.

CONTENTS

LIST OF TABLES

This study was mainly exploratory, and several different data-collection techniques have been employed. Specifically, information was obtained from the following: (a) interviews with black students, (b) a survey of black (and white) students, (c) forums conducted by black students, (d) written documents and records concerning campus activities, and (e) interviews with the black advisor on each campus.

The study was designed to facilitate a comparative analysis between black and white students attending two-year and four-year schools that are supported by public and private resources and which are located in cities and small towns. This analysis is basically the combined experiences of black students in all four schools.

In our study, there has not been a systematic testing of hypotheses because of the absence of an accumulated body of information about black students on white college campuses. Thus, the primary goal was to provide a body of verified information about a little-understood situation.

In August 1969, letters written by the study director were sent to administrators of fourteen colleges and universities in New York State. The study was described, and the preliminary interest of the school in participating in the project was sought. Favorable replies were received from twelve institutions. Several were quite eager to cooperate and expressed the hope that such a study might assist them in finding answers to the perplexing problem of how to relate to the increased number of blacks on campus. Four colleges were selected that facilitated the kinds of comparisons mentioned. The number was limited, so that a variety of research methods and techniques could be used. It is especially important to diversify data-gathering methods in an exploratory project. Before students were approached, on-site interviews were conducted with administrators who represented the president of each of the four colleges. The administrators were asked to designate a member of the college staff with whom we could have continuous conversations. In all instances, we were referred to the black advisor. We then asked the black advisor to introduce us to an important black student on campus. The black student was then requested to introduce us to a black group from whom we could seek permission to conduct the investigation.

The research planning staff consisted of a study director, an assistant study director, and a field coordinator. They identified themselves with the disciplines of sociology and psychology. Interviewers were nine male and female, black, brown, and white graduate and undergraduate students in journalism, law, education, and sociology. A new and important role was that of the campus consultant. He or she was a black student on each study campus who was recommended by the black advisor. The student consultant compiled a census of black students on his or her respective campus, organized and tape-recorded the campus forums semimonthly, and attended research staff meetings two or three times during the course of the year. Telephonic communication was maintained with the student campus consultants during the interim.

In-depth interviewing of black students continued throughout the school year on all four campuses until prematurely terminated in the late spring by the student strike that affected all of the study campuses. These interviews were lengthy and somewhat open-ended—although several questions were routinely asked by all interviewers—and were based on questions generated in weekly staff discussion sessions. Interviews conducted early during the school year focused uniformly on a limited number of issues and were recorded topically. As the study progressed, more topics were included. During the latter portion of the study, interviews ceased entirely to be recorded topically and were recorded in a narrative fashion. At the close of the study, the interviewers were asked to code the narrative material by selected topics and themes, to assist in the analysis.

The population for the interview portion of the study was, theoretically, all of the black students on each of the four campuses who were U.S. nationals in either undergraduate or graduate programs. The sample, in actuality, was those black students who could be located and who were then willing to participate in the interview. Students to be interviewed were initially informally contacted by project staff as they were encountered on the campuses. Later, as lists of the names of the black students were supplied by campus consultants, appointments were established for the interviews. There were few refusals; cooperation was widespread.

Interviewer style varied. Some interviewers preferred informal discussions; some preferred more formal question-answer periods focused on specific predetermined topics. Some interviewers took notes during the interview, some taped the discussions, and still others wrote up the interview from memory soon after it was over. While accuracy and detail were required and direct quotes were preferred, pressure was not exerted on the interviewer to either interview or record in a style unnatural to him. Two interviewers, one black and the other white, were retired from the study team because of difficulty in establishing relationships with the students or difficulty in recording details of the interview. The quality of the interviewing was monitored continuously.

Assignments were made so that each interviewer spent a day a week on each of two different campuses. The net effect was to have three different interviewers on each of the four campuses for one day a week. It was hoped that this assignment pattern would facilitate coverage of campus events during different periods of the week, invite comparisons between campuses in staff discussions, and minimize a possibly distorted view of a campus due to the bias of a single interviewer.

A second primary source of data for the study came from a questionnaire survey of a sample of black and white students conducted after spring vacation during the second semester. The survey questionnaire was composed of a series of items concerning the student's opinion of student rights, the student's impressions of classroom activities, the student's impressions about himself, and the student's report of the extent of his interracial contact. Specific questions had their origins in written reports of interview findings, previously conducted research studies, and questions and issues raised in staff meetings.

Letters were sent to each sample member during the week preceding the survey. The letter indicated the purpose of the survey, where and when it was to be conducted, and stated that an honorarium was to be paid for participation. Letters were sent to all black students from whom names and addresses were available and to a proportional random sample of white students from each of the four study campuses. It was felt that a letter addressed to an individual would have a greater chance of conveying the purpose of the study and the importance of participation than other approaches we considered.

Study staff members administered the survey at each of the campuses. The survey was a monitored but self-administered questionnaire, which took approximately one hour to complete. Participants came to the announced place, filled out the questionnaire, and then signed a "tear sheet," indicating to whom the honorarium was to be sent. The tear sheet was removed when the questionnaire was returned, assuring anonymity to the respondent. Most respondents preferred that the honorarium be sent to them rather than to a charitable or social action group.

After the first week of survey administration, the tear sheets were checked against the name lists of students to whom letters of invitation had been sent. Students on the list who had not participated were sent a second letter indicating that an additional opportunity would be available two weeks later.

The completed questionnaires were coded as to campus, race, and sex of the respondents, and each was assigned a sequence identification number. They were then keypunched, according to predetermined IBM card codes. The data were then processed by the SPSS statistical package at the Syracuse University Computing Center.

Of the persons invited, 49 percent actually reported and filled out the questionnaire. Approximately forty black students did not have a second opportunity to respond to the survey questionnaire, because the schools were disrupted during the strike, and it was difficult to make follow-up contacts.

The third major source of data was a forum of black students established on each of the study campuses. These convened approximately twice a month for six months. The purpose of the forums was to provide an opportunity for black students to explore a number of diverse issues among themselves. Some of the issues were presented by the campus consultant, who convened and moderated the meetings, while some were raised and discussed spontaneously. It was assumed that information developed out of an interaction situation might be different from data obtained by interview. Forum members were dinner guests of the study project at a restaurant of their choice before each discussion session. The forums consisted of approximately ten black students from a given campus who met regularly for dinner meetings. Selection of forum members was delegated to campus consultants and/or black advisors.

A tape recording was made of the meetings. Typescripts were produced from the tape. Copies of some of the typescripts were sent to the campus consultants to be examined for accuracy. As with the interviews, forums were analyzed for thematic content and examples were drawn from the materials that were illustrative or recurring themes.

Various materials sent to students before arrival on campus were examined. In addition, materials such as the campus newspaper, the alumni bulletin, and catalogs were collected, especially if they presented characterizations of the "black experience" on campus.

To obtain an understanding of the campus context from another perspective, the black advisor on each campus was interviewed extensively. The interviews were conducted by either the assistant study director or a consultant anthropologist. These interviews were conducted in late spring.

All of the methods and techniques described were valuable and helpful in revealing what it is like to be black on a white college campus. The different kinds of data were correlated for our final report.

The students attended four colleges that were located in three different communities. The communities were selected to facilitate study of the effect, if any, of the presence or absence of a local black population and of community size on the adaptations of black students. The colleges made possible comparisons between two-year and four-year institutions and publicly supported and private colleges.

Little Village, New York, was incorporated as a village in the first quarter of the nineteenth century. Six decades later, its population was 700; it now approaches 2,000. Situated on a river in a region of small farms, Little Village is still very much a country town. Yet, it is not totally isolated: the state turnpike is only a half-hour away; Metropolitan City, New York, lies thirty miles to the northwest. Through the center of town runs U.S. 007, the old Western Highway, which still carries some traffic between Capitol City and Frontier City.

The college is a unit of the State University of New York (SUNY) system. Founded at the beginning of the twentieth century as an agricultural school, it was absorbed by New York State after World War II and rechristened an agricultural and technical school. The campus comprises 150 acres of land, running southward from the center of town. In 1969, enrollment totalled 1,800 students, majoring in twenty-six fields, including agriculture, business, nursing, engineering, journalism, and allied vocational areas. Also included in the roster of programs is general education, intended primarily for those planning to transfer to a four-year college.

Little Village College shares with other SUNY units an immense expansion program, begun in 1962 and just now nearing completion. A new library, student union, administration building, dormitories, laboratories, an infirmary, and athletic facilities are to be in use by fall 1971. Student organizations abound: there are music and drama societies, a student government, Greek-named fraternal organizations (but no fraternity or sorority houses), a student newspaper, and a radio station.

Academically, Little Village College students can assume a fairly relaxed posture. During his first semester, a student need only maintain a 1.00 grade-point average (in a 4.00 system). As to graduation, a C average overall is the stated requirement.

Other areas of student life are more rigorously administered. Little Village College adheres to a compulsory attendance plan, in which three absences constitute a cause for disciplinary action. Female students have curfews and are required to attend weekly dorm meetings. All students under twenty-one years of age must reside in campus dorms or with parents. The campus is "dry," save for special events sanctioned by the president of the college. Gambling is prohibited.

The cost of education is relatively low. Total costs, including tuition and room and board, seldom exceed $1,700 per year. Moreover, most students receive some form of financial aid. State University scholarships are available, as are work-study programs, guaranteed loans, and Education Opportunity Grants (EOG's). Black students are given special financial assistance, which provides from $1,900 per annum. In many cases, both black and white students receive two years of education at little or no expense to the student.

The Little Village admissions staff has recently been self-consciously aggressive in recruiting blacks. Of the forty-two black students admitted in 1969, thirty-six remain. Most are participants in the EOG program and enjoy a sizable amount of financial aid. In 1969, black students demanded their own union and a course in black history. It is now college policy to assign dorm rooms "black to black" unless otherwise requested. Black involvement in campus affairs is minimal.

Like Little Village College, the college in Small City is also a unit of SUNY. Previous to the 1960's, the school was exclusively engaged in teacher training; now it is a four-year liberal arts college, with a germinal graduate school. Small City College is rapidly acquiring all the accouterments of large American universities: among these are an 1130 IBM computer, a biological field station, and a mammoth library. Only three of the thirty buildings now in use existed two decades ago.

The community of Small City, New York, has a population of 23,000. Although the size and status of the community have diminished since the turn of the century, its lake shore location makes it an important port, which can receive seagoing ships. A number of small industries and a very large power company provide much of the local employment. Many residents now commute nearly fifty miles to work in Metropolitan City, New York. Small City, New York, is old: traders and fishermen began a settlement there as early as the first quarter of the eighteenth century. There is, therefore, some urban decay but also one finds a good deal of civic pride. Many old structures have been refurbished and kept operative and in good condition. Ethnically, Small City is like Gaul, easily divisible into three parts: white Anglo-Saxon Protestants, Italians, and Polish residents, in order of ethnic population size. The number of blacks is miniscule.

The academic curricula at the college conform to the pattern set by most liberal arts colleges. The division of arts and sciences offers majors in most of the standard areas (e.g., physics, history, literature, economics, French, and so forth). There are also divisions of industrial arts and technology, vocational technical education, and graduate studies. Still very important is the division of elementary and secondary education. Many senior faculty are professors of education, and large numbers of students pursue the education curriculum.

The student enrollment currently stands at 7,200. Many of the students are local residents of the area and commute to school from home. Academic standards, while not overly rigorous, are reasonable: a 2.00 average (in a 4.00 system) is required for good standing throughout a student's career. The usual spectrum of undergraduate diversions are present. Fraternities and sororities (without national connections), dozens of clubs, student publications, athletics, and musical organizations just begin the list. Like most other SUNY units, Small City College is a "residence campus"; only those over twenty-one, commuters, or those living in Greek houses are exempt from the dormitory requirement.

With a dormitory room comes an obligatory board contrast, plus some rules that apply to proper conduct in residence halls. The girls' curfew is 1:30 a.m., except on "special occasions by approval." Freshmen living in the dorms cannot own cars. The college permits alcohol only at "registered social functions."

As in all SUNY units, the cost of education is reasonable. Undergraduate tuition is $400 per year. Yearly expenses, including tuition, room, board, and personal necessities total about $2,000 to $2,300. Financial aid is available from the college, state, and federal government. EOG money is also available; New York State Regents Scholarships are competitive but generous. College aid is given on the basis of "need, academic ability, and citizenship." There are no athletic scholarships.

Out of 7,200 total enrollment, sixty-eight black students attend Small City College. The sex ratio among black students is just about fifty-to-fifty. All but seven of the blacks live on campus. The total number is small, but for the 1970 school year, plans have been formulated to recruit 200 black freshmen. Staff has grown in proportion: the history department has a black professor who teaches an Afro-American course, and personnel has hired two black men, one in admissions, another as a program director.

Black students generally room together in the dormitories, but there is no college policy regarding room or roommate assignments. In the middle of the 1969-70 school year, blacks were given their own lounge in the student union building. Apart from this, there is no de jure separatism at Small City College. In 1969, there was a great deal of talk about a separate black quad, but it has not materialized.

The two final colleges in this study—Cosmopolitan College and Metropolitan College—are located in Metropolitan City, New York, which has a countywide population of nearly 500,000. Metropolitan City became prominent at the beginning of the third decade of the 1800's, when the Cross State Canal was completed. Subsequently, the extension of rail lines and the discovery of valuable minerals engendered high-speed urban growth. Today, Metropolitan City is at the junction of the state turnpike and the interstate route. Several different kinds of industries employ thousands of laborers, skilled workers, and white collar and management personnel. Cosmopolitan College is the largest single employer in Metropolitan City.

Unlike Small City and Little Village, Metropolitan City, New York, has a sizable black population, between 5 and 10 percent of the countywide total. The old black ghetto was somewhat dispersed by urban renewal. Blacks are scattered in small concentrations throughout the community's southern and eastern sections. Metropolitan City's ethnic populations include large numbers of Irish, Italians, Poles, Germans, and Jews.

Metropolitan College is a two-year public school. It was founded in the 1960's and presently offers twenty-one two-year associate degree programs, including computer programming, business administration, and dental hygiene. The college is housed in a downtown office building. Plans have firmed for the construction of a new twelve-building campus with a projected enrollment of 4,400.

Current enrollment is 1,750 full-time and 1,785 part-time students. Of these, sixty are black. There is no campus housing, nor are there plans for any. All students are "commuters." Total cost per year for a county resident is $480, not including books and other personal expenses. For many students, this cost is deferred or eliminated by EOG money, student loans, a law enforcement education program, and other special aid programs. Financial assistance also comes from local professional and social organizations. Cash awards are given to certain students in chemistry, dental hygiene, nursing, and other fields. A work-study program also provides financial help to some students.

The number of black students, though still small, has doubled in the last year. A search has begun for a black faculty member, thus far without success. A social science course dealing with black history is being developed; the English department gives a course in American Negro writers, which is taught by a white man. As of 1970, the Metropolitan College staff included one black advisor.

Situated on what locals call "the hill" is Cosmopolitan College, one of the largest private educational institutions in the country. Founded during the last third of the nineteenth century, Cosmopolitan College, once connected with a religious domination, is now thoroughly secular in orientation. Enrollment stands at 16,000 students, 6,000 of whom are in the graduate school. Within the undergraduate population, there are 214 blacks. To catalog the college's academic curricula would be impractical. Suffice it to say that Cosmopolitan College offers the full spectrum of undergraduate majors in liberal arts, engineering, education, business, drama, art, music and has seventeen different schools that offer graduate education. Likewise, student organizations abound: fraternities, sororities, publications, sports, clubs operate at the level one might expect in a college of this size.

High tuition and living expenses (approximately $3,950 per year) effectively limit the number of lower- and lower-middle-class students in attendance. Yet, financial aid is available from many diverse sources, and many students spend four years at Cosmopolitan with the assistance of a scholarship. Cosmopolitan College grants over $1.75 million in aid per year.

Cosmopolitan College is a residence campus. This means that the college has invested millions in dormitory construction. More than two dozen residence units are maintained by the college. Undergraduates must be twenty-one or over and have a satisfactory academic standing to apply for a housing exemption. Such an application may then be approved or rejected by the dean of students. Until 1969, Cosmopolitan College was a "dry" campus, with traditional curfews and separation of the sexes.

The black students are a small but growing—and vocal—minority. They receive from 20 to 30 percent more financial aid than white students. Blacks at Cosmopolitan College are conspicuous in campus politics. Cosmopolitan College has a black student union, a black studies program, several independent black organizations, nine faculty members, and two black administrators.

The small number of black students on all of the college campuses included in our study was even smaller just one year earlier: 42 percent are in their first year of college. This proportion is more than four times greater than the proportion of fourth-year black students on campus, three times greater than the proportion of third-year black students, and about one and one-half times greater than the proportion of second-year black students. Most students are eighteen and nineteen years old.

For the most part, black students attending the white colleges included in this study are northerners. The homes of nearly three fourths are located in northeastern states, and slightly more than two-thirds spent their childhood in this region of the United States. Only about 10 percent of the parents of the black students who were investigated now live in the South.

The black students come from families of varying size. They are more or less equally divided between small families consisting of one or two children, three- or four-child medium-sized families, and larger families of five or more children.

Sending children to college often requires that both mother and father work. Of the mothers of black college students in this study, 80 percent are gainfully employed.

The black parents with children in white colleges, like those included in our study, are striving to provide opportunities for their offspring, which many of them did not have. Of the mothers and fathers of these black students, 66.6 percent did not attend college. In fact, 33.3 percent never graduated from high school, and almost one out of every ten of the black parents failed to complete an elementary school education.

Yet, their children dream no small dreams. Of the black students in the four white colleges, 72 percent hope not only to obtain a bachelor's degree but also to do graduate work. Whether or not they will be able to fulfill their aspirations is still an open question. Their financial resources are small, scholarship assistance is still limited (45 percent receive no financial aid from the school), and other problems are plentiful. For example, nearly two-thirds (64 percent) report academic performances at the C level; only one-fourth (23 percent) say they get grades of B and above.

In summary, the black students at the white colleges included in this study—a high proportion of whom are in their freshmen year— are northern-born youngsters who come from families of limited educational achievement and modest economic resources. The gainful employment of both parents is usually required to send their offspring to college. While most of the black students receive some financial assistance, many do not. These students tend to have high educational aspirations.

Black Students
at White Colleges

1

BLACK SEPARATISM
OR
WHITE RACISM?

Black separatism is a function of white racism. It represents failure in the relationship between the black individual and the white society. The black experience at a white college is a story of hope, frustration, and disillusionment. It is a story of acceptance and rejection. It is a story of individual and institutional racism. It is a story that is important to every member of the community.

Consider the experience of Catherine (the name is fictitious), a black coed on a white campus. Her feelings are representative of those expressed by many of the other black students interviewed for our study. She has opted for separatism. By exploring the adaptations of Catherine to the stresses of a white environment, we may better understand some of the causes and consequences of the separatist movement that has emerged among young black people and the larger black community in its relationships with a white society.

Catherine is a third-year student who grew up in a middle-class family in a middle-sized industrial city in the mid-Atlantic region of the United States. Here is what she said about her family and her three years on a white college campus:

> I come from a complete Negro family [consisting of my mother, my father, and one sister]. My mother was always actively involved in civil rights [organizations] and she was involved to the extent that it took her out of the home quite frequently. As a child, I didn't understand this.
>
> She used to try to instill in my sister and me some . . . sense of what it [is] to be black. I would say to her

that she was one of those fanatics like Malcolm X. [I would say to her] "white people really aren't like that and black people really aren't in such bad condition." I came to this school [in 1967] with that attitude.

Only . . . this year [1970] have I really started thinking about the kind of education I am getting. The first two years, I came here as a gung-ho freshman [and sophomore]. People weren't that militant when I came here in 1967. I think it was still the hope of many black people to get into the American mainstream.

. . . I came and I remember I decided on purpose not to send my picture [to be attached to] the application after I was accepted. They put me in a hall with 500 girls, all white except me. My roommate was from [the South]. It just so happens I did get along with my room-mate. You could call her a liberal. She wasn't the type liberal who jumps up and down and tells you she's had these dealings with black people. . . .

In this type of situation, being . . . isolated, I began to get into the system of having mainly white friends as my good friends. . . . To a certain extent I was getting involved in a lot of white activities. . . . I was pretty much with their social bag. I didn't go out with any white guys. . . . I used to eat with the girls on my floor but the other black girls [who ate in the same dining hall] wouldn't join me when I was with all those whites. . . .

Little incidents started happening. My white friends would make some mistakes in what they'd say and do. They would hurt my feelings. But I would take into account that they were really my friends and sometimes they do make errors. We used to always study together for exams in one course. The content for one exam was about prej-udice and poverty. They didn't call me in when they were studying. When I found out they had already studied and did not include me, I asked why and was told that one of the girls said Negroes were inferior and the other girls said they thought it wouldn't be right to include me in the study session after that type of attitude has been aired.

Then Martin Luther King died and a lot of places began to be burned and a lot of those liberals—when the fire got nearer to their doorsteps, a lot of attitudes started coming out. Around this time, the Union of Black Collegians got to be more active. I began to make a break there and began to look at myself and this so-called friendship. Ever since then, I've been developing more intense attitudes about myself and people. I am a completely different person now than I was when I was a freshmen and I think it's for the better.

Someone once said I had to go to a white [school] to find out I was black. And that is exactly what happened to me. The majority of my childhood was spent with middle-class black people. When you're in a system where you don't see the oppressor and you don't have to come into contact with him all the time and you are middle-class [which means] you're not struggling every day for survival, you tend to forget exactly what's going on. But when you are put into a situation like I was where you're only one out of 500 and every day you're exposed to some kind of racism, whether subtle or blatant, it begins to work on you.

Most of my friends now are black. The social situation? Objectively, it's better [than at some schools]. But because of the fact that I'm a junior, I'd say it's worse. When I first came in 1967, there weren't nearly as many blacks here as now. We were confined to a very small group of black people. What happens here for the girls, since there is a small number of blacks is this— once they're out of the freshman year, they're on the shelf. . . . By the time you're a sophomore you're old blood. Everyone knows you, whom you went out with, what you're like, what you're doing, what you're not doing, whether it's worth your time or not. By the time you're a junior, like I am, you feel like you're a mother towards them all. . . .

Where am I on the political spectrum of activism? I don't believe I'm all the way up the line to radicals and revolutionaries. I have a very intellectual viewpoint about that. I don't believe I'm ready to get out on the street. . . . I don't think I have the courage to go out there. But I can say that revolution is the only way. I can't say I'm a complete revolutionary. I'd say I'm in the process of becoming one, maybe. I'm very near that point of total involvement.

. . . the only reason I can say we might have a revolution is because nothing in the past has worked. Revolution on a full scale is something we haven't tried. . . .
I suppose that, for a young person, I have some pessi-
mistic views about the future.

We are in three divisions among the black students
here: there's the bookworm who doesn't participate to
any extent: there's the social group that can go either
way: and then there's the political activists. About 15
percent are political activists; about 10 percent don't
participate; and 75 percent, the rest, are in this twilight
zone.

The black women [are thinking about] pushing for a
Black Women's Living Center. . . . We want to get these
pockets of black students out of these all-white dormitories and get them into a house of their own. The sororities and fraternities do it; why can't black people live
together? Let's face it. Black people are just more
comfortable with black people. I don't particularly like
being questioned about my hair or style of life by white
people. There are certain foods I like to eat which this
school ignores or can't cook. Secondly, it would be a
unifying device to get everyone together in a living situation. To me it's only natural. Before coming to [this
school], I came from an all-black community and it's
natural for me to live in one. . . . Of course, those who
raise arguments against it don't say or may not realize
that . . . unification is a threat.

Interracial social activity? It's going on but it has
decreased by almost 100 percent since my freshman year.
My dormitory situation now? There is no other floor
like it. There are six blacks on the floor—all in a row.
The rest of the floor is white. . . . We went to the Dean
of Women and told her that we are necessarily put in a
environment that is frustrating because we are black
students, that we are all good friends, that we need each
other. Since the Dean of Women had seemed to slow
down the plans for a Black Women's Living Center we
didn't see why it would be that much of an inconvenience
to give us six rooms on a floor together. She did. . . .
She didn't want to precipitate an incident. . . . She also
could have seen that we did have a legitimate gripe.

People talk in revolutionary terms [on campus] but I'd really like to know what they're going to do. . . . I don't see revolution. . . . If not revolution, I can't say what we should do. I don't stop trying to plant the seeds that would bring about revolution, such as making people aware, unifying them, making them proud, making them have the mission to go out and put down the oppressor. I'm suggesting that I might not have the faith that the goal [of the revolution] will be reached.

The institutions in society are [so] strong. The CIA [Central Intelligency Agency] is everywhere. I believe that America desires to perpetuate concentration camps for political opponents to the system of this country. People who speak out against the system are being systematically cut down—Eldridge Cleaver, the Chicago Seven, the Black Panthers. I wouldn't say that this society is against all-out genocide for black people.

My mother is pleased at my transformation [and even a bit awed] because now I am more militant than she is. My father has very definite positive ideas and feelings for blacks. He doesn't have misconceptions. He believes that anyone given the opportunity will oppress you.

Going away to school . . . has a lot to do with creating revolutionary blacks. Hometown is small with a lot of middle-class blacks. They are in their own little world and caught up in it—not being able to escape that world and see something different.

Black Studies at this school is long overdue. I'm glad we're finally putting very important elements of history and art back where they belong. We are finally beginning to educate ourselves, and, I suppose, others to the fact that black people are, in essence, really beautiful. . . .

I feel that everyone shouldn't go into Black Studies. If you feel that something is wrong with the American system as it is and you feel that Black Studies is a way you can learn something about yourself and do something with it, like going back into the black community and teaching others what you have learned—then by all means—take Black Studies.

I'm really opposed to having whites in [Black Studies]
classes with me. . . . . I suppose that if there are some
whites who really are dedicated to the ideals of equality for
all, I suppose there are some whites that a little more
education wouldn't hurt. . . . . I can't be getting hung up
worrying about educating white students [now]. I feel that
the less classes I have to be involved in educating whites
the better. I can move faster. I'm not on the defensive.
Psychologically it's just a much better atmosphere [with-
out whites around].

The role of black professors and counselors is increasing. This is the first year we've had this many
black professors and counselors on campus. Many of
them will be moving out of their various departmental
offices and into our Black Center. They will be there for
counseling. Yes, it will make for a much closer relationship. We are really looking forward to that. We are
starting our own free university which will deal solely
with black topics and will be open to only black people
and in which black professors will be available to lead
discussions. So their role has definitely increased.
We're educating ourselves. They're educating us in
history and we're educating them to radicalism.

This is an important case study of a black student who has
experienced a radical transformation from an integrationist to a
separatist within the period of three years. Catherine attributes her
transformation to the racist experiences she encountered in school.
"I had to go to a white [school]," she said, "to discover that I was
black." She made this discovery because of the ridicule, rejection,
insensitivity, and insincerity of some whites. She now feels that her
major source of protection is a radicalized black experience that
excludes whites. Moreover, her new mission in life is to radicalize
others.

Catherine came to college very much in the tradition of all
boarding school students—trying to break away from family control.
She rejected her parents' negative assessment of whites and dis-
approved of her mother's intensive social action efforts on behalf of
blacks. She had a positive concept of herself and of her race. She
believed that black people could compete, that black people were
beginning to make it, that their condition was considerably improved.

Although coming from a racially segregated residential neighborhood in her hometown, she deliberately opted for an integrated living arrangement on campus. She learned through direct contact with her white roommate that all whites are not insincere. At least one white person was trustworthy.

However, Catherine also learned by direct experience that acceptance as an individual is no guarantee against rejection because of one's race. Rejection by white members of the study group was a decisive experience in her life; it convinced her that many whites are untrustworthy and insincere. The tension of racial conflict was introduced into the study group by a white member, yet the group decided to deal with the tension by rejecting the black rather than the white member. This was a racist solution. The black student was innocent of any wrongdoing or tension-producing activity. If exclusion of a group member was the only way the group believed it could manage racial tension, shouldn't the white member who introduced the tension by expressing the insulting remark have been excluded? Instead, the group excluded the victim of the prejudice. Incidents like this one multiplied and became a series of insults for Catherine. They were danger signals to her and, in large part, were responsible for her withdrawal from frequent interaction with whites.

Campus life, of course, is part of the larger society. Hostilities in communities throughout the nation are reflected on campuses. When the apostle of nonviolence, Dr. Martin Luther King, Jr., was murdered, blacks then knew that some whites had no respect for any black person, that no blacks were safe and secure in this society. For Catherine, illusions about racial acceptance and racial integration vanished. Dr. King, a black man, was shot by a white man. This fact did not escape black people, including Catherine, and helped to justify the separatist movement as a form of protection. Racial integration was viewed as a risky alternative. Smoldering embers of optimism and a willingness to give whites the benefit of the doubt were snuffed out when Dr. King was killed. Idealism turned into despair. Although the black unity and separatism promoted after Dr. King's death was primarily a defensive move, Catherine admitted that her interest in black unity could become a means for aggressive revolutionary activity designed to bring down the present system, since no other approach to justice seemed to work.

Blacks on college campuses are striving for a genuine sense of community, wherein they would be held together for reasons other than external threat. The concern with Black Studies is one indication that blacks are beginning to develop a sense of significance of themselves as a people with a unique heritage, independent of their involvement with whites.

The Black Student Center, which may have served initially as a place where blacks could retreat from the insults and abuses of racism on campus, is now becoming a unique presence of the black experience in the college community, where black art and other aspects of black culture may be exhibited. Moreover, black student organizations on white college campuses are becoming potent political forces, placing their representatives in strategic positions in the governance of the total school. Thus, an increasing function of black unity on campus is to serve as a power base for inducing change in the organization and structure of the total college community. Catherine showed some awareness of this new function when she said, "Those [whites] who raise arguments against [black togetherness] . . . don't say or may not realize that . . . unification is a threat."

A final example that the black separatist movement is concerned with issues other than the threat of white racism is Catherine's observation that separate facilities for blacks on campus would facilitate their participation in black cultural experiences.

Catherine's experiences indicate that there is a confidence gap in the making between the races on college campuses. It seems to be widening year by year, as the races come into closer association with each other. As interactions between the races increase, trust and confidence between the races appear to decrease. Perhaps, increased interactions have canceled all illusions of justice and fair play and have revealed the racist orientations of many whites.

Withdrawal of the security and support of white campus groups from blacks, such as the study group for Catherine, is a type of rejection. Withdrawal from participation in white campus groups by blacks is a type of protection against the recurrence of stress due to rejection. To the extent that the separatist movement among black students is a type of withdrawal, it may be characterized as a response to the threats of racism, rejection, ridicule, and arbitrary behavior.

Withdrawal, of course, is not the only adaptation one can make to stress. Cooperation or compliance, aggressiveness, and withdrawal are the three basic kinds of adaptations. Cooperation and compliance

may free the distressed individual from the forces causing the disturbed emotions and thoughts, or may permit the continuance of the
forces, or may lead the individual to blind submission, in which he
is unable to take care of himself.[1] Withdrawal due to stress in the
environment may protect the individual from some of the forces
causing the disturbed emotions and thoughts and enable him to survive
until conditions improve, or may permit the continuance and increase
of the disturbing forces, or may lead to extremes of selfishness and
unreliability.[2] Aggressiveness, another way of dealing with stress,
may stimulate the individual to take decisive actions that will free
him from the stress-producing circumstances or may lead the
individual to confused and violent action that is inappropriate to his
ultimate goal.[3]

Cooperation with whites was the way Catherine attempted to
eliminate any racial stress in the campus environment. Despite
her participation and cooperation with white members of the dormitory
study group, for example, she was not freed from the stress-producing
experiences of racial discrimination. It is fair to say that her cooperation and compliance possibly facilitated the continuance of attitudes
of prejudice by whites and the distressing circumstances of discrimination. The absence of confrontation delayed the process of attitudinal
examination required of prejudiced whites.

Not finding solace and security in white groups, Catherine increasingly turned to blacks for the support that she and any student
needs and must obtain. Her increasing experience of ridicule and
rejection by whites, the death of Dr. King, and the organization of
several militant black student groups were confrontation experiences
that caused her to examine her attitudes and actions toward whites.
Following these events, as she put it, "I began to make a break . . .
and began to look at myself and these so-called friendships" with
whites.

Catherine justified the withdrawal from whites on three counts:
(a) she was protected from daily exposure to "subtle or blatant
racism," (b) she found her association with black people "more comfortable," and (c) she was able to deal intensively with issues relevant
to blacks without "getting hung up worrying about educating whites."
Apparently, her sojourn in the white dormitory left her unconvinced
that blacks and whites need each other. Indeed, the conclusion that
she has formed as a result of her interracial experience is that
whites believe blacks are expendable.

Withdrawal is likely to free the campus environment from the
stress of racism only if whites realize that they need blacks and are

willing to change to maintain an association. With this kind of awareness, whites will interpret the withdrawal of blacks as rejection and
will feel aggrieved and distressed over the break in the relationship.
They could then be moved to rectify the wrong that contributed to the
termination of association. Without such an awareness by whites,
withdrawal by blacks may facilitate the continuation of racist behavior
by whites.

The withdrawal of blacks also may be understood as a type of
rejection of whites by blacks. Usually, the message of withdrawal
by blacks is garbled and unclear, due largely to the inability of whites
to understand it. Whites may interpret the withdrawal of blacks as
their desire to be with their own kind and "do their own thing."

Some blacks, presumably being tongue in cheek, have stated
that the black separatist movement is meant to protect whites as
well as blacks. Harry Edwards has stated that black students have
tried to avoid subjecting whites to ethnocentric styles of behavior,
dancing, conversation, and attire that they may not appreciate or
identify with and which they may regard as derogatory, vulgar, or
uncouth. This is one of several justifications, he states, why blacks
have advocated separatism on the predominantly white college
campuses.[4] Many whites have accepted this ready-made interpreta-
tion and have adopted it conveniently as their own.

The tangle of pathology in race relations in America is most
clearly seen on the college campuses, where whites reject blacks
and blacks reject whites. They both declare that their actions of
withdrawal are without malice and hatred but are designed to protect
the welfare of the rejected race. Under these conditions, withdrawal
hardly could be expected to relieve the stress of racism on campus.

Therefore, if withdrawal is ineffective, then aggression is
likely to be the next stage of adaptation. Already, Catherine is
becoming more aggressive. Of herself, she says, "I am a completely
different person now than when I was a freshman." She goes on to
explain how she has changed. "I can't say I'm a complete revolutionary. . . . I'd say I'm in the process of becoming one, maybe. . . ."
Catherine's assertion that revolution is the only way indicates that
both cooperation and withdrawal have failed to relieve the stress of
white racism.

Other black students like Catherine are moving through a
series of adaptations. Some may be in the cooperative stages, others
in the withdrawal stage, and still others in the aggressive stage. It

is well to view these stages as a series or as a continuum on which
students may move back and forth according to their experiences.
Thus, progress is not automatic from one stage to the next. The
progression from one stage of adaptation to another may be interrupted
at any time by eliminating the stress that is disturbing to black students.

The movement of Catherine from cooperation with whites to
withdrawal and toward aggressiveness is directly attributable to the
fact that the stress of white racism did not abate during the first and
second stages of adaptation. She is tending toward aggressive radicalism now because other kinds of adaptation did not work. The
student questions whether revolutionary activity will relieve the
stress of white racism. But her doubts do not deter her from attempts
to radicalize others, because nothing else thus far has been effective.

Black separatism cannot be understood apart from the circumstances and conditions of life created by whites for blacks. However,
an adaptation such as withdrawal, though originally a response to
racism, may take on a life of its own and seek to perpetuate the
special arrangement of a community of like-minded and look-alike
people. Thus, the National Advisory Commission on Civil Disorders
had reason to warn Americans that if the stress of white racism is
not eliminated, soon this nation could divide permanently into two
societies—one black and one white.[5]

Because black separatism, as explained by Catherine, is indeed
a manifestation of white racism, this should neither be encouraged
nor opposed by whites. What should be opposed is white racism.
Any group has the right to withdraw from active participation with
others if withdrawal is the only available way group members can
protect the integrity of their personhood against insult and assault.
As stated by Alexander H. Leighton, sometimes withdrawal can
"enable [the individual] to survive until conditions improve."[6] The
withdrawal of black students is an adaptation to white racism designed
to protect them against ridicule and rejection. The encouragement
by whites in the college community of this black separatism is
acknowledgment of the presence of racism on campus. It serves as
a signal to white students that the college does not intend to oppose
it but will facilitate ways of avoiding as much unpleasantness as
possible by those who are victims of the stress.

Whites who encourage black separatism (which is a response
to white racism) are like the white members of the dormitory study
group who excluded their black member to protect her from prejudice.
Separation may temporarily aid blacks who are victims of the prejudice,

but it does nothing in the long run to change the oppressive attitudes and actions of whites.

To facilitate the separation of a college campus into black and white enclaves, without, at the same time, eliminating the racism that contributed to the separatism, may have unanticipated consequences, for which administrators must assume responsibility if they encourage the process. To facilitate withdrawal into racially homogeneous associations may be brutal. Although separatism may provide psychological relief from white insults, it renders blacks vulnerable to white assaults. Hostile and mutually exclusive racial collectivities eventually will take retaliatory action against each other. The bombing, firing, and vandalizing of Black centers on a few college campuses are indicators of more evil to come. An identifiable and separated black minority in the presence of a hostile and encompassing white majority is like a sitting duck, inviting much mischief.

The alternative arrangement of enforced black and white togetherness does not offer a happy solution either. To insist that blacks remain in the presence of whites who deliberately insult them is to induce frustration and rage, which may lead to violent confrontation.

All of this is to say that the basic black-white issue on the college campus is not black separatism but white racism. Of course, it is easier to facilitate black separatism and more difficult to oppose white racism, but our analysis should help save the members of the campus community from false choices. We believe that eradication of expression of white racism will eliminate the need for black separatism.

NOTES

1. Alexander H. Leighton, The Governing of Men (Princeton, N.J.: Princeton University Press, 1964), pp. 263-64.

2. Ibid., p. 256.

3. Ibid., p. 266.

4. Harry Edwards, Black Students (New York: The Free Press, 1970), p. 71.

5. National Advisory Commission on Civil Disorders, Report (New York: Bantam, 1968).

6. Leighton, The Governing of Men, p. 265.

The black experience at a white college is isolation and rejection, as illustrated by Catherine's story, if blacks depend on
whites only. Blacks, like other students, need individuals, groups,
and institutions to turn to for solace and support. Since support
from whites is not dependable, blacks increasingly are turning toward themselves. They are not risking friendships with whites,
which they often find fragile and unstable.

Therefore, white colleges that deliberately recruit black students must enroll at least a few hundred or be guilty of condemning
a small number of blacks on campus to an inadequate social life and
intraracial as well as interracial discord. The quality of campus
social life for blacks is directly related to the number of black students enrolled and not to the ratio of black and white students.

We found that the social life of most blacks on white college
campuses tends to be limited to interaction with other blacks. Almost one-half (43 percent) reported not having been in a racially
mixed social group in the six months preceding the survey. Further,
three-fourths reported that their participation in interracial parties
was rare or only an occasional experience. Nearly three-fourths of
the black students (73 percent) reported that almost all of their closest
friends were black.

The actual experience of racial exclusivity tends to exceed the
students' expectations. For example, 66. 6 percent of the black students expected to have parties only with other blacks, while, in reality,
75 percent said the parties they attended were all black. Also,

15

only about one-fifth of the black students said blacks should date only blacks. However, we found that slightly more than 50 percent dated only blacks.

We also tried to assess the quality of social life on campus for black men, compared with black women. Our study offered a modest opportunity to explore whether black coeds experienced more difficulty adapting to white college campuses in the area of dating than black men, or vice versa.

Not only the quality of the social life but the entire black experience on white college campuses is conditioned by the number of black students enrolled. The size of the black student population has two functions—one political and the other social. As stated by Ormand, "Being a member of the Afro-American Association was a matter of survival." He felt that the college, figuratively, puts the blacks aside in a little corner, where they are lost when only a few are on campus. "Now the story is different," he said. Through increased numbers, unity, and organization, blacks have been able to achieve increased political power on campus.

Black women probably more than black men are concerned about the number of black students on campus for social purposes, although black men, too, report that they would derive social benefits from an enlarged campus black population. A larger number of blacks on campus would increase the range of personalities available for social interaction.

When their number is small, dating is a serious problem for black students on white college campuses. The chance of a black person finding another black person with whom he is compatible is more limited on a white college campus. Any extraordinary personal feature may compound the difficult situation. A woman in her thirties, for example, who attends a college with a black student population of less than seventy-five, calls the campus social life "a living hell." She describes her plight this way, "I am an old lady compared to the guys in school and they don't want no part of me and I don't want anything to do with any baby." Whenever possible, she leaves the campus on the weekend. The story is repeated by another student who is a tall girl and, therefore, has few opportunities to date "because there are so few tall black guys on campus." She goes on to say, "When it comes to dating, some will be left out and the chances of such is greater when there is a small group, as all black brothers and sisters are not compatible."

Even when there are no extraordinary circumstances, such as age or height, to set conditions on the date-selection process, the interaction experience between black males and females is filled with tension and uncertainty when there are only a small number of black students on campus. When two black students find they are compatible and have much in common, it is a joyous experience. However, the joy is tempered by anxiety that, by chance, the small black population on campus may not yield another similar person if the existing relationship should ever end. Thus, one date may press another prematurely for an exclusive relationship. Black men, especially, place a high value on maintaining their freedom and a premium on not getting "trapped" into exclusive relationships before they are ready. Consequently, some of the black women experience what they have described as a lack of involvement and the absence of commitment on the part of the black men with whom they associate.

Several black students also build a strong case for more blacks on campus to overcome the competition among men for the attention of the few black women whom they consider attractive. Being unsuccessful in the competition with other men for the most sought after college dates, and fearful of becoming entangled beyond the point of extrication in a relationship with the available but less-popular dates, some black men withdraw entirely from the campus scene and seek a "safe" relationship elsewhere, off campus—that is, a relationship with a person who is less elusive and less demanding.

The complex problem of achieving a satisfactory social life when the number of blacks on campus is small is summarized in this series of students' statements.

There aren't enough blacks. . . .

. . . . .

I'll be glad to get out . . . .

. . . . .

A little social life would be best. I don't know many of the girls, only a couple. The rest are conceited and stuck up and act like they are Miss Black America. I dated Betty once; she was nice. But she kept calling me up. I don't want a girl like that. I date a girl [off campus in a nearby town now]. . . . I see her pretty often; she keeps me satisfied so I don't get too uptight.

Stating the problem succinctly, from the female perspective, Majorie said: "We don't have much social life here at school. We don't have dates." Blacks on campuses where there are only a few tend to withdraw and turn away from, rather than toward, each other socially.

We cannot determine from the data available how many black students at white colleges go off campus and out of town weekends to find dates. However, it is clear that many—men and women— yearn to go. "If someone says there's a dance in [a nearby city], we go, man," said Winslow at Little Village College. "I usually leave the campus every weekend."

Another consequence of too few blacks on campus is summarized in a down-to-earth fashion by a black freshman. Jackie says: "Socially I don't like it at all because there are so few black people here. You are used to seeing the same bunch and after awhile you get tired of seeing the same people." Essentially, she described a small black student population as "a dull scene."

The small number of black students on white college campuses also eliminates anonymity. The dating process is facilitated if all dates do not always know all other dates. When dating among black students is limited to other blacks on campus and when the number of black students is small, it is difficult to keep information about who goes with whom from becoming community property. Reputations have a way of traveling ahead of the maker in a small, closed society, interfering with new dating opportunities. "By the time you're a sophomore, you're old blood. Everyone knows you, whom you went out with, what you're like, what you're doing, what you're not doing, whether its worth your time or not." So the call for an increase in the number of black students on white college campuses is a call for enlargement in the range of personalities available for social interaction.

The black student population on the four campuses in our study range from approximately 40 to 200, out of total student enrollments of 2,000 to 15,000. On each of three campuses, however, there were few black students, less than 75, in the total student body. A standoff relationship between men and women, complaints about dating, and concern over compatibility are less often issues or topics for discussion on the campus where the black enrollment is relatively large. Moreover, there is much less off-campus activity when the black student population is substantial.

Clinton, a twenty-one-year-old junior, in describing the cooperative relationship between blacks when the enrollment is approximately 200, said: "The people who participate [in black affairs] do so for different reasons. This is mainly due to differences in personality. I don't feel there is any big clash; we have people that fit at every point. . . . " Without explicitly emphasizing the importance of numbers, this student declares that the "greatest benefit" of college for him has been, "meeting more [black] brothers and sisters, and getting to know a lot of them."

Another student at the same school makes this assessment of the campus situation: "Up until this year, I don't think there was a black experience on this campus. But . . . now black students are providing more of their own things that they can get into." The Black Center was pointed out as one such opportunity where they may hang out together. The student who voiced a feeling of comfort in having a facility like the Black Center said that 95 percent of his activities were centered around the campus. This experience of campus-centered social life differs from the off-campus activity at colleges where the black enrollment is relatively small.

While complaints about the social life are less frequent and less severe on a campus with a relatively larger number of black students, 200 is not enough to still all feelings of disgruntlement due to an insufficient range of personalities with whom to interact. Though not a prevailing view, this complaint is mentioned by enough students to merit attention.

If you don't go to the familiar places like the inn, the movies and the black parties, then there is actually little to do. And at these places, you usually know everybody. In a racially isolated situation like ours, you usually start all relationships on a brother-sister basis, where you know all about each other and take each other's feelings for granted. It's sort of a Peyton Place here. After awhile, it gets depressing and you want to get off campus. You want to alienate yourself from the black community. . . . It's an immature environment in which all is known and all relationships are somewhat artificial.

While this student feels that other blacks get too close to him for comfort in the closed black society at Cosmopolitan College, some blacks have found the relatively large number of 200 or more students and the many different black organizations a welcome relief from previous settings they have been in, in which there were few, if any, other blacks present.

Initially, we thought that there might be greater polarization among blacks on campuses with larger black populations and greater cohesion among blacks where their number was small. Our assumption was that there would be more and different kinds of organizations on campuses with larger black populations and that conflict would be engendered among the students due to competition between various black organizations for their support and allegiance. The data do not support this expectation. Actually, there is less cohesion and more tension among black students at white colleges where the black student population is relatively small.

Neither black nor white students are joiners. Only about one out of every two are active participators in an established campus group. Student government appears to be one of the least attractive activities. Only 7 percent of the black students and 13 percent of the white students admitted to even working in a student body candidate's campaign. Blacks seem to be more able to mobilize and deal with issues that directly affect their lives. Protests and demonstrations are the usual methods of mobilization. During the course of the school year, 48 percent of the blacks, compared with 23 percent of the whites, said they had participated in one or more groups that demonstrated or presented a formal list of complaints to the faculty or administration. While the rate of participation in protest activity by black students was twice as large as that found among whites, these activists were slightly less than a majority, which means that a great many campus blacks, as well as their white counterparts, are inactive.

The blacks pressed into action tend to work largely with other blacks. Only 15 percent of the black students in our study had worked as a member of a racially mixed action group. The fact that blacks tend to work only with other blacks may be due to choice as well as to other factors: 66.6 percent of the black students believe that they ought to have the privilege of working as individuals within any group they choose. Despite this feeling, only 15 out of every 100 black students on the combined four-college campuses have had such an interracial cooperative experience in the area of social action. Consequently, 80 percent of the black students at white colleges in our study now assert that they should work together as a separate united political group to effect changes in their schools.

Usually, the students work through such groups as the Union of Black Collegians, Student Afro-American Society, and Black Student Union. The black groups have different names on different campuses but tend to perform similar functions—stimulating black awareness, facilitating black unity, and obtaining programs and facilities for black students on campus.

On all campuses, the newly formed black organizations, such as those mentioned above, have spearheaded the drive for Black centers and black housing. Such groups also have led the fight for the development of a program for Black Studies. Black awareness grows out of group discussions on the writings of black authors at organization meetings and through the collective analysis of racist practices at white colleges and the meaning of these for blacks. Also, these groups have sponsored black speakers on campus.

The recently organized black groups have been reasonably successful in achieving all of their goals. Particularly have they negotiated well with the administration of white colleges in obtaining facilities for Black centers and in establishing Black Studies programs.

Problems in developing unity and internal cohesion within the black organizations continue and are due to several factors: (a) jockeying for power positions, which is a common experience in newly established associations; (b) a tendency for the "true believers" to attack blacks who are not active participants in the black organizations; and (c) conflict about organizational goals—political versus social and particularistic versus universalistic. Most students recognize that the black organizations are both social and political; some wish to emphasize one over the other, which sometimes leads to a hassle. The experience of being accepted immediately in the black organizations is meaningful to some students. They also like the opportunity of seeing other blacks at meetings of the organizations, and they enjoy the black parties that grow out of these repeated gatherings. The more politically oriented black students like some of these activities too, but many see them as a waste of precious time. The particularistic-universalistic conflict is related to the social-political split in definition of group functions in that many students are satisfied that blacks now are meeting and doing things together. The gathering of blacks, then, is an end in itself. Others are concerned with bringing blacks together as a power base for negotiating with white institutions on specific issues. Actually, both goals are being fulfilled in the black organizations on white college campuses. But the struggle continues as to whether the particularistic goals should take precedence over the universalistic goals until a crisis occurs, which tends to unite all sectors. White administrators and faculty members seem to be adept in precipitating crises and in consolidating the campus black community.

It is fair to say that the social and political life of black students at white colleges would suffer were the Student Afro-American Society, Union of Black Collegians, Black Student Union, and other similar groups to disband. Whites appear not to comprehend this fact: approximately 70 percent in our study state that they are indifferent or opposed to the proposition that blacks should work together as a separate united political group to effect changes on campus. Yet, only 13 percent of the white students in our study have worked with blacks during the school year in racially mixed social action groups. Despite white protestations against black separatism, whites are not working with the blacks. The black students at white colleges sense that they are on their own, and they have proceeded to organize. When the black student population is sufficiently large, by chance the few blacks who participate in organized activities and associations may link up with others who have compatible interests; under these circumstances, groups may continue and fulfill the needs of black students, although the interests and participation of specific individuals may wane from time to time.

Since the college campus is a densely populated settlement of heterogeneous individuals who are interdependent in an organic way, it seems appropriate to consult community theory to help explain the structure and process of interaction and social organization among its members. Several years ago, Louis Wirth pointed out in his famous essay on "Urbanism as a Way of Life" that the relationships between people in a community are directly affected by the number of inhabitants. He said that if the number of inhabitants of a community was increased beyond a few hundred, this phenomenon was sure to limit the possibility of each member of the community knowing all the others personally.[1] In terms of our study, an increase in the black student population from 75 to 200 or so seemed to be associated with an increase in freedom, flexibility, and some degree of anonymity when desired in social relationships. Harvey Cox, influenced by Wirth, called anonymity a liberating phenomenon, which " . . . helps preserve the privacy which is essential to human life."[2] Wirth explained that most relationships in a community are secondary rather than primary, which is to say that they are impersonal rather than personal. Anonymity, then is one device that protects one from excessive personal claims by others. Indeed, it would be oppressive if all members of a small, closed, and isolated community had total access to, and knowledge about, each other. Such action surely would encroach upon personal freedom and social flexibility.

On campuses where the black populations are relatively small and the social life of their members is limited to interaction with other black students, these populations are found to take on the character of extended families. When this occurs, all relationships, including those that might otherwise be secondary, become overly personal. The black students who make unlimited claims upon each other find such relationships supportive at times, but also stultifying and confining. The temptation to turn a black student community into an extended black family is increased when the number of black students on campus is small. Thus, it is necessary to enlarge the black student enrollment on any white college campus beyond a yet undetermined number (but certainly over seventy-five) as a means of protecting black students from turning all of their associations into a brother-sister affair.

Harry Edwards has stated that small black student populations foster tightly knit cohesive black communities on white college campuses. [3] Our findings indicate that very small black populations on white college campuses merely give the appearance of a tightly knit cohesive community.

Mary Lou, at Small City College, where the black enrollment is less than seventy-five, summarized the attitude of many of the other black coeds:

The black students are okay. I use to associate a lot with them but I don't associate that much anymore because I am tired of seeing the same faces.

I'd just like to see more black guys. The guys, they are few. Everyone has their disappointments: you do like one, then you don't; there's no one else particularly you like.

There just has to be more people so that when you wake up in the morning—particularly for girls—you can think that 'maybe I'll meet my special someone today.' But when you know everyone who's on campus, [you say to yourself] 'Why put on make-up? Who am I trying to impress? I know everyone who's here.'

It wouldn't make any difference [going out with someone white] but they're not asking us out. There are one or two black girls here who go out with white boys and quite a few black boys who go out with white girls.

The sisters are playing for keeps and the guys just

want to fool around. If a [black guy] goes out with a black
girl, she might want to get serious or something like that.
That's not exactly true [but that's the way the guys see it].

Girls like to go out once in a while for a date and
dress up and have a nice time and to go to a really nice
place. I did it a few times.

There ought to be a study of the psychological effects
of going to a school where there are [a few] black people.
I think I've been affected mentally here. It's no joke!
I get so depressed. I don't cry or anything. But I get
very depressed. There's nothing to do about it. I don't
study or anything. The first part of the semester I was
doing well and studying but now I'm dropping. Now I'm
so sick of this school. I go around and don't feel like
doing anything.

It's really a beautiful campus. It really could be
a great place if there were enough [black] people. The
trouble is psychological for the girls 'cause they don't
have anyone to take them out.

Ruth, an eighteen-year-old freshman from a large metropolitan
area who attends the same school, has adapted fairly well to the
poor dating situation and spends most of her free time with girlfriends
in the dormitory. Nevertheless, she confessed disappointment. "I
always had the idea that you go to college and get your education and
that the social life is also a high point. But it's the only thing that
bothers me really. "

Emily, a senior who comes from a large family, demurs when
asked if she would recommend that other blacks go to a white school.
"Hard to answer that question, " she replies. "The hell I've gone
through I don't know if they could stand it. It took something within
me to continue. " Although the black population on campus is still
small, she finds the increasing number "very encouraging. " She
interacts with other black students and describes these relationships
as "lots of fun. " Knowing that other blacks are around gives Emily
a feeling of security. She believes that black students care about
what happens to her. She does not limit all of her associations to
blacks, but reports that most of her friends are black. After nearly
four years of college and some interracial associations, Emily still
declares, "I find it difficult to trust whites. " The frequency of this
or similar statements by black students on white college campuses
is striking.

A first-year black coed attending a school where the black
enrollment was less than fifty describes the campus experience as
"terrible" because she sits in her room all weekend. Some men at
the same school complain of having nothing to do and sitting in their
room. Apparently, such men and women do not know about each
other (very unlikely), are shy, or find each other's company incompatible.

Cleveland, an eighteen-year-old student at Little Village College
(a very small black enrollment), frankly admits that there is a
cleavage between black men and women. He does not elaborate, but
his remarks clearly indicate that all is not well between the black
brothers and sisters on campus.

One black male said that a campus with less than fifty black
students has "a vacuum of social activities for blacks." He would
like to see more outlets for black self-expression and a center for
black cultural and social activities. One suspects that such a place
might also serve as a setting for casual meetings between men and
women.

The men at Metropolitan College agree that meeting black
women on campus is a problem. Some feel that the coeds act as
if they are "higher" than the men and give the appearance of not
wanting to associate with them. Harold said the black girls say "hi"
and "bye" and "stuff like that" but do not give any indication of
wanting to establish a deeper relationship. At this college, there
are more men than women black students among the few who are enrolled. Due to circumstances described, the men tend to withdraw
from the dating game and often attribute their lack of interest either
to their own standards ("The few girls don't look so hot") or to the
standards of the girls ("They're snotty").

Black men on campus are not totally without female companionship. There is some interracial dating, mostly black men and
white women. Many reported that interracial dating was frequently
an uncomfortable situation, due to pressures exerted by black and
white students. As stated by Ralph:

It's too much of a problem to date a white girl. . . .
We just go to someone's apartment and listen to records
and fool around. It's too much bother to go any place,
like to the movies or anything. My uncle just sold me
his car, so now I have wheels. If I went out with whites
I would have a hassle. It wouldn't be worth it.

The black men students are aware that many of the black women, and some men, disapprove of their dating whites during a period when blacks are striving to achieve more unity. Therefore, they tend to limit or curtail interracial social activities as a way of maintaining cohesion. As stated by one student, black-white dating goes on, but the blacks are expected not to "flash it around" and certainly not to take a white date to black parties. Celeste said "interracial dating makes my jaws tight." She is embittered when she sees interracial dating because, in her words. "White chicks have an advantage over the sisters. Sisters must compete for the black guys, white chicks don't have to. She has her man and whenever she wants to, she comes over and raids the black woman's territory, something not freely available to black women." Essentially, this black student placed the initiative for interracial dating upon white girls rather than upon black guys. An implication is that black girls might not be as uptight about interracial dating if they had equal access to "white guys," although several black girls insist that they would not accept dating invitations from whites. Most black girls who reported that they would date whites say that they are seldom asked for a date. "The white boys are afraid of us," observes Mitzi.

The lack of interracial dating may also be due to the pressure against integration in the black student community. Wanda said some blacks consider it to be "the absolute worst thing if you interracially date." The negative connotation associated with interracial dating is expressed by a series of derogatory tags attached to the participants. The black women call black men who date whites "Uncle Toms" and the black men call the females who date whites "honkey lovers." The pressure against interracial dating, however, is unequal for women, as compared to men.

While black men set forth all kinds of justifications for their interracial involvement, including exploitation, an expression of freedom, or a bridge for racial reconciliation, they are rather stern in their admonitions against interracial dating for black women. Reservations about interracial dating are expressed by black men in various ways, like Wilson, who calmly said, "The black guys don't particularly care too much for that" (meaning black girls dating white boys). Another, more violent, reaction: "I'll wring your neck if you go out with that white boy." To all of this, the girls respond, "Golly, that isn't fair." They sense that they are victims of a double standard, which may further contribute to the black male-female estrangement on white college campuses. Of the black women on white college campuses in our study, 71 percent date only blacks, compared with 36 percent of black men. The proportion of black men who interracially date is twice as great as that for black women. Our data indicate a stand-off relationship between black men and women on these campuses, especially where the black enrollment is small. Black men seem to have greater access, compared with black women, to companionship and social activities. Thus, black women experience more difficulty in social life than black men in adapting to white college campuses.

NOTES

1. Louis Wirth, "Urbanism as a Way of Life," American Journal of Sociology, Vol. XLIV (July 1938), reprinted in Paul K. Hatt and Albert J. Reiss, Jr., eds., Reader in Urban Sociology (New York: The Free Press, 1951), p. 39.

2. Harvey Cox, The Secular City (New York: The Macmillan Company, 1965), p. 40.

3. Harry Edwards, Black Students (New York: The Free Press, 1970), p. 179.

3

**HOUSING
AND
LIVING
ARRANGEMENTS**

Whether or not black students should live apart from white students in their own housing is a controversial campus issue that has not been resolved by students or school administrators. Black students argue persuasively both for and against all-black dormitories.

Three of the four colleges included in our study have dormitory facilities. The regulations pertaining to housing are similar on all campuses. Some 80 to 90 percent of the undergraduate students live in college housing or college-approved housing. A campus residence usually is required for students under twenty-one years of age, unless they are living at home, with other relatives, or are working in a private home for room and board. Students other than freshmen have the privilege of choosing their roommates. When possible, student selections are honored.

We do not know the number of black students who request black roommates. However, 66.6 percent have lived with other black students all or most of the time they have been in college. And 20 percent have lived with whites only. Despite the fact that two out of every three black students room with other blacks, as a group, they are undecided as to whether blacks should have a separate dormitory: only 28 percent affirm that black students should. The remainder say that they should not have a separate housing facility (41 percent) or that they do not care (32 percent).

It is indeed remarkable that some black students still are willing to try racially integrated living centers in view of their reports of many insults. Though not a universal experience, several black students have been greeted at white colleges with unfriendliness.

Two students from the same hometown said this, "When we arrived [on campus] right away we found the kids to be unfriendly." Others give specific illustrations of unfriendliess, insults, and insensitivity by whites. Ginny tells this story about her interracial dormitory experiences.

> The white girls didn't know what to say [to me] since they hadn't been around Negroes. They asked silly questions that were, and are, annoying. [Then there were] slips of the tongue. For example, one of my good friends said, 'Eeny, meeny, miney, moe; catch a nigger by the toe . . .' We were both real embarrassed, but she especially.

She goes on to say that it may help race relations for her to live in an interracial dorm but that it doesn't help her personally. She states that she needs a closer relationship. With white girls, she contends, "it is hard, if not impossible, to get a close friendship" going. Other black students relate incidents of discourteous behavior, such as whites staring at them and constantly asking questions, like: "What is your hair made of?" "How can you tell when you have the measles?" Black students term these "silly" and "insulting" questions.

Theresa, a freshman, and Irene, a sophomore, tell why they refused to participate in a dormitory Christmas skit written and planned by their "good friend," who is white. The girls said their dormitory floormates wanted them to play Santa Claus and Mrs. Santa Claus. Irene said,

> We didn't think anything of it until we saw the script for the skit. I was supposed to stand there like an idiot and my [roommate, Mrs. Santa Claus] was supposed to hit me and say a whole lot of stupid things. I was supposed to have something on my behind and they were all supposed to run over and throw boxes at me. It looked like Amos 'n Andy junk. That's why we didn't do it. The [white] girls [on our dormitory floor] were angry with us because we decided not to do it. But I didn't care. I thought it was dumb. On another floor, the [white] girls wanted a black girl to play Snow White. They thought it would be cute . . . maybe their intentions are nice. But what comes out really gets to you.

Sandra, who is a member of a family in which the parents are professionally employed and who has lived in an integrated residential neighborhood, states that she finds her dormitory, where she is the only black student, uncomfortable. As she puts it, "[I] get very tired of being the oddity in the dorm."

Another student recounts an experience of blatant rejection in the dormitory when she met her "big chum," an upper-class student who was supposed to help her get settled as a freshman. She and her "big chum" had corresponded with each other during the summer, and the exchange had been pleasant. The black student was happily looking forward to meeting her new friend on campus, only to be rebuffed as they met for the first time in the freshman dormitory, when the "big chum" exclaimed with dismay—"You're a nigger!" Needless to say, there was never a second meeting.

June, twenty-three years old, has moved out of the dormitory, partly because of her age but also because of her experience. She describes dormitory life as "hostile." However, she attributes the failure in her relationships with whites mainly to her impatience and unwillingness to persevere. In a reflective mood, she said:

> I guess if I had worked at breaking through the shell of
> whites and their stupid curiosity about blacks I could have
> made it, by taking time, explaining everything about me
> that was different down to the smallest detail. But, like
> who needs it? I couldn't see that it was worth making
> friends with 17 stupid white chicks on my floor. I dealt
> with the situation with a hostile attitude. I explained
> things by telling them it was none of their damn business.

Another black female is not quite so adamant; however, she expressed resentment over the fact that all of the white girls on her floor come to look when she does her hair. She feels as if she is a learning experience for whites on campus.

Some blacks, who have experienced insult piled upon insult from whites, are now turning the tables and trying their hand at the nefarious art of the cruel "put down." Althea, who shared an apartment with whites, tells about her hassle in keeping the apartment clean. "No one was cleaning up and taking out the garbage," she said, "and the place was terrible." Althea said that she cleaned up for two weeks but that her actions got no response. She said that she wondered if the whites were not used to doing work for themselves and expected blacks to do all of the housecleaning. One evening, when Althea was visiting with an African friend in the apartment and discussing among other things housekeeping problems, she discovered that the African student was having similar problems with her white apartmentmates.

Speaking at a conversational level but loud enough to be overheard, Althea said, "The way one keeps one's living quarters reflects upon one's background and home training as a person." Though not a party to the discussion, one of the white roommates must have overheard. Althea reports that her white apartmentmate immediately left her company, whom she was entertaining in another section of the apartment, took out the garbage, brought up the vacuum cleaner, and began cleaning. Althea said there has not been any housecleaning trouble since the evening of that direct communication.

Maurice, whose father is a policeman, says:

Man, the dorm is all screwed up. Kids just don't give a damn about anything. We are having fights over the way the lounge is kept. We blacks can clean the place up at night before going to bed and by the next morning the place is a mess. This is done on purpose. If we could catch the guys doing it, we would kick some asses.

Matthew, who had been initiated into a white fraternity, relates a story of insensitivity. A fraternity brother had traveled extensively in the South during the summer and had taken many photographs of people and places. One photograph was of several Negro people in a relaxed and leisure-time setting. When it was flashed on the screen during an after-dinner showing, one of the fraternity brothers with a guffaw-like outburst yelled, "Look at those lazy niggers." He suddenly realized that the black fraternity brother was present and apologized to him for making such a remark in his presence. Matthew said he was disgusted because his white fraternity brother apologized for disparaging black people in the presence of another black person but not for holding the disparaging attitude.

In the light of these experiences, we understand better why nearly three-fourths of the black students on white college campuses say that almost all of their closest friends are black. Even so, a considerable number of black students would like to try to establish friendships with whites and to live in interracial housing on campus. Some of these students have experienced a real breakthrough of the racial barrier.

Elsie, a freshman who has lived both in the North and in the South, is in a suite of rooms on campus consisting of three blacks and five white girls. Of her roommates, she says: "We have really good race talks, telling [the whites] exactly how it is to be black. None of the [whites] had been around blacks or talked to blacks. It's

a good experience for us to live with whites." Again, the theme of a
learning experience intrudes. But in this situation, blacks and whites
are mutually learning from each other. Thus, none feels put upon.

A black athlete has two roommates, whom he describes as nice.
A freshman with a mixed racial ancestry has one black and one white
roommate. She describes both girls as nice and says that she gets
along great with them.

Our study indicates that some black and white students are able
to communicate and form enduring friendships. However, our general
impression is that there has been a breakdown in communication.
Black and white students engage in little dialogue and, therefore, have
limited understanding and involvement with each other.

Some blacks are assuming leadership roles in their dormitories,
like a junior (with a private school secondary education) who is president of her dormitory floor and a nineteen-year-old black sophomore
(whose parents have graduate degrees) who was secretary of her floor
last year and now is secretary of the dormitory council. These students
exhibit a "take charge" attitude and a certain amount of confidence in
their own abilities, perhaps promoted by their backgrounds.

Some of the conflicts in the dormitories are psychological and
situational, rather than racial. For example, cliques form among
black students, which tend to divide them. Black students living in
different dormitories get identified as separate groups. Felix, a
nineteen-year-old transfer student, has a white roommate by choice.
He says that they get along well together because they like the same
type of music—soul music. Felix had a black roommate at another
school with whom he did not get along. On the other hand, another
black student says that he prefers to hang out with blacks because he
and other blacks like soul music, which whites cannot understand.
Obviously, this black student has not experienced a relationship with
a white person like Felix's roommate. Because he has not had such
an experience, he has assumed that all blacks and whites have incompatible tastes.

Oscar, a sophomore from a large metropolitan area, middle-
income family, feels that there should be more opportunities for
black students to live off campus so that they can get away from what
he describes as "the suppressive atmosphere of this white-oriented
campus." At the same school, Roger, a senior with professional
parents from a large metropolitan area, also wants to get an apartment off campus. He finds the black experience on campus and the

pressure for blacks to associate only with blacks a "depressing" and "sickening" environment. The fact that each of these students wants to move off campus for opposite reasons in terms of racial association demonstrates the situational and psychological dimensions of the adaptations of black students at white colleges. Therefore, it is probably impossible to develop a single racial solution in housing that will be acceptable to all of the black students on white college campuses.

Our data indicate that white students have little interest in the problems that trouble black students, like racial oppression. The relationship between black and white students on campus is seldom a topic of discussion among white students when they get together. Only 5 percent of the whites frequently discuss this issue, compared with more than two-thirds (68 percent) who seldom or never talk about race relations at the college. The whites on campus are a little more inclined to talk about distant problems, like the racial situation off campus; even then, their interest is miniscule, with only about 10 percent frequently discussing this topic.

We found that whites oppose any move to separate blacks from them by placing all blacks in a separate dormitory facility. Only 2 percent believe that blacks should have separate housing. An overwhelming majority—nearly nine out of every ten white students—are against an all-black dormitory. This orientation by white students creates a puzzlement for blacks. Although many whites say that they want blacks to be near to them and to share dormitories and other housing, they apparently do not wish to share the burdens that trouble blacks. It is as if whites want to be physically close to black students but distant from their social and personal concerns. It is a situation of whites wanting to deal with blacks on the terms of whites. The black students sense the hypocrisy of this approach. In our interviews, they often talked about the "showcase nigger" that whites collect and install to prove their liberality.

Blacks, like other students, talk about dating, sports, music, politics, the war, and plans after college. But, in addition, black students frequently discuss the racial situation both on and off campus. They are vitally aware of the problems of oppression. It is the introduction of this topic that divides black and white students. Whites' lack of expressed interest in the problems of discrimination causes the blacks to proclaim that they and whites have nothing in common.

Under these conditions, some black students insist that it is better for blacks to live apart from whites. Three different patterns of separate living for black students are beginning to emerge on white college campuses: (a) all-black roommates (b) all-black sections within dormitories, and (c) all-black dormitories. Of the black students, 75 percent have lived with other black students all or most of the time; this fact indicates that a considerable amount of racial separation already has taken place. Several campuses are approaching the second pattern of all-black sections within dormitories; the third pattern is an open and hotly debated one among blacks. The weight of evidence to date appears to be against this kind of living arrangement, but not overwhelmingly so.

With reference to all-black sections in dormitories, Alex, a campus leader, said: "[We] blacks usually hang around our rooms. . . . We intend to remain as apart [from whites] as possible in our dorms." As Catherine reported earlier, there is no other floor in the dormitory like the one she lives on. The six blacks on her floor all have rooms in a row and the rest of the floor, consisting of twelve more girls, is white. Catherine points out that another dormitory on campus has the same arrangement, and even a higher ratio of blacks of whites on the particular floor. How strong will be the pressure in the future for the reservation of racial sections within otherwise white dormitories cannot be determined.

The third pattern for racially separate living, the all-black dormitory, brings us back to the issue raised at the beginning of this chapter. While the proportion of black students who definitely believe that blacks should have separate dormitory facilities on white college campuses is a minority—a little less than one out of every three—this proportion could rapidly increase were most of the black students who presently "don't care" (32 percent) won over to the way of thinking of the separatists. Were there an increase or continuation of incidents of insult and insensitivity, as described earlier, we believe the undecided would join with the separatists.

Already, there is evidence of much concern among campus blacks over the issue of racially homogeneous housing. On any campus, one can obtain opinions that vary all the way from doubt to strongly held convictions for and against an all-black dormitory. If all blacks were living in the same dorm, Juanita conjectures: "We would be able to do things better and have better communication. A lot of people say that the black dorm wouldn't work because of the cliques among the blacks." An opposing view was voiced by Melinda at the same institution:

> If all black girls on campus lived together, that would
> cause many problems. Every [black] girl on campus

doesn't get along with [all black] girls. There are whole
groups that don't get along. Dating possibilities would
be awful. It would have to be a small group that would live
together because definitely there would be a lot who
wouldn't want to. I wouldn't live there at all.

Probably the best summary of the indecision of black students
as a whole about all-black dormitories on white college campuses
comes from a tape recording of an informal discussion of black girls.
Excerpts from that discussion follow:

I don't really think that a black dormitory is right for the
women because there would be too much competition . . .
seeing that there are only a few black guys on campus.

. . . . .

What has the competition for the guys got to do with living
in a black dormitory? You have conflicts with women over
men whether or not you live with them. I don't think that
would be a hassle.

. . . . .

I don't think a dormitory for black girls is right because
there are too many personality differences on campus.
Like when you look at whitey, they just barely make it;
and with us separated, we barely make it. So, like, with
all of us in a dormitory, I don't see how we could do it.

. . . . .

I live in a suite where there are only three girls and at
times it's a hell house. So I can imagine what it would
be like if there was an entire floor. Throughout history
women have never gotten along and I just don't believe
that black women, being the way they are, could make it
with an [all-black] dormitory.

. . . . .

I also live with a black girl, and we also run into quite a
bit of difficulty due to personality conflicts. . . . Most of
the girls here come from many different backgrounds and
it's more difficult for us to adjust to one another . . . .

. . . . .

You find many of the white girls pretending that they like
each other, when they really can't stand each other's guts.
Whereas, with the black girls, they tend to more or less
let each other know how they really feel about each other.

. . . . .

When [black] women live together not only do they form
personal feuds, they also become dependent upon each
other . . . just to get along. So if you're in a dorm by
yourself, you tend to be more independent. Also, there is
less conflict with other [black] women.

. . . . .

I disagree that we tend to become more dependent on each
other. [The black girls I live with], we're friends, but, if
I had to, I could live without them. . . . The implication
was that [black women who live together] become so
dependent upon each other that they can't live without each
other.

. . . . .

I didn't mean that [one black girl] becomes so dependent
on another that she cannot survive a day without her
[roommate]; but you do have a tendency, for example, if
you are going out to really want somebody elso to go out
with you. And you have a tendency to get into the function
of a twosome or threesome rather than necessarily doing
something on your own.

. . . . .

[The black girls I live with], we like to be together. Its
true that we do have fun together. I depend on them too.
But I don't think that we sorta hang on each other all the
time.

. . . . .

[This idea about black girls being dependent on each other]
sort of conflicts with the idea that [black] girls could not
live together because they couldn't get along.

. . . . .

[Some of the black girls I live with now I get along with]
because we have things in common and we think in the
same terms; whereas with one of the girls, we don't get
along because we don't have anything in common. Now
as far as a black dormitory goes, she would be one of the
persons who would make it a disadvantage, and, like, I
feel it wouldn't work.

. . . . .

[I live across the hall from a black student now]. We don't
live with each other. In a black dormitory, we would be
totally surrounded by blacks. We would have no whites to
break up our monotony at times. [Our dormitory now] is
not totally black and I think that's one of the reasons why
we [blacks] get along. . . . If I lived around the blacks on
this campus, as far as the girls go, I know that I'd be
fighting 24 hours a day. It's true.

. . . . .

I agree 100 percent with those remarks. [I'm on a different floor from most of the blacks in my dormitory]. I
like my privacy. But I want to be able to talk to some
blacks, to get up and go someplace to talk to them, or to
have them come to visit me. But I think that in a dormitory
situation we'd be in and out of each other's rooms, using
each other's things, getting in each other's way. Somebody
would want to study; somebody would want to play the record
player. As close as we are, I don't think a black dormitory
would work out well.

. . . . .

I don't see why a black dormitory has anything to do with
privacy. Even though I have a black roommate, we get
along pretty well, because she does her thing and I do
mine. And, like, we never have any disputes about how
the room is kept or anything else. Besides, she's not
around very much; so that gives me more time for
privacy. And when we want to go out, if we want to go out
together, we go; if not, we go our separate ways.

. . . . .

I'd like to ask, if living with a white girl—what privacy
do you have? Like, you're staying with a black girl, you
want your privacy, but, like, with white girls, you have
even less privacy.

· · · · ·

I think I'd have more privacy with a white woman, even
more, because with a black roommate I discuss a lot of
things. If I were with a white girl, I probably would just
say 'hello' to her in the morning and nothing else and I
wouldn't discuss black issues and what we were doing in
class or anything else. I'd probably be in my room studying most of the time or going out to visit the other black
kids.

· · · · ·

I have a white roommate and I don't relate any of my
business to her at all because she can't get totally involved in it and I don't feel it's for her to know. Whereas,
with a black roommate you may occasionally; . . . but with
her, my white roommate, I have more privacy and everything. The most I say to her is 'goodbye' on my way to
my classes and when she comes in she'll say 'hello' and
that's all there is to it.

· · · · ·

If I had to live with white girls, I'd rather live off campus
somewhere by myself. . . . Even though there are a lot of
conflicts living with black girls, life is much better living
with black girls [as I now do] than living with white girls.

· · · · ·

I think I would have more privacy living with a white
girl. . . . With a white roommate, if you don't want her
to know, you don't tell her; she asks no questions and you
can still live together, I think, under normal conditions.
You can't keep a black out of your business on this campus,
because they are involved. I know because I live with a
black busybody.

· · · · ·

If you had a white roommate, you wouldn't have to worry
about your business being put out among black people. But
you'd never know what she'd do among whites.

. . . . .

Well, who is concerned about whitey. I don't give a goddamn
what they think!

. . . . .

I had a white roommate who was awful. It was like living
with an ironing board. You just said hello to her in the
morning and goodbye at night. This year I have another
white roommate and we're a little closer but still, you
know, there are things about me that she doesn't know and
I'm sure that there are things about her I don't know.
Next year, I'm going to live off campus and I think probably
the kids I'll be living with will be white because of the
privacy I'll have.

. . . . .

I believe that you can't have privacy with anybody—white
people or black people! Some blacks tell the whites more
about their business than they do the niggers.

. . . . .

I'd like to refute that statement. . . . Like, I come from
a ghetto and I know I don't want nobody to know my business.

. . . . .

About the only difference as far as having a white roommate and a black roommate, as far as privacy. . . . I
don't think that you have any more privacy with a white
roommate than you would have with a black roommate.

. . . . .

I think that the only difference is that you might be able to
scare the hell out of the white roommate whereas you
might not be able to get your bluff as far with the black
girl.

. . . . .

Catherine, a black leader on another campus, tal.s about the growing possibility of an all-black house for women on her campus.

> A black women's group was organized to give women a
> voice. Nobody knew what radical demand to make. So
> everybody decided that the women had to ask for a Black
> Women's Living Center. The black men supported the
> demand of the black women, except that the men didn't
> really want a Black Women's Living Center at the time.
> But I think things are beginning to change. I'm sure we
> could get 20 girls [out of the 100 or so on campus] who'd
> like to live in a Black Women's Living Center, maybe
> more.

We see the three patterns of racial separatism in housing for black students as a direct manifestation of their lack of trust in whites. This distrust is a consequence of the betrayal, insults, and insensitivity that blacks have experienced on white college campuses.

As things presently stand, about three out of every ten blacks on white college campuses definitely believe that blacks ought to have a separate dormitory. Maybe two or every ten blacks would live in such a facility. In the light of these findings, we conclude that the black roommate and the black section in a white dormitory are presently more acceptable living arrangements for blacks on white college campuses than is the all-black dormitory. Yet, things are changing and changing fast. These preference patterns could change if racism continues uncontrolled on white college campuses. The more radical innovation of a separate dormitory may be demanded.

4

BLACK STUDIES

Blacks insist on the immediate application of knowledge to the solution of community problems. They believe that a Black Studies Program will accommodate this interest, that it will be less theoretical and more pragmatic, that it will deal with real and relevant issues. A few black students perceive the Black Studies Program as a protective suit of armor, insulating them from a hostile white environment. They are fearful of being whitewashed in other courses designed and taught by whites.

Working with people rather than with things is important to black students. Of our black students, 70 to 75 percent indicated they are oriented to occupations that involve working with people.* This is reflected in their choice of majors. (See Table 1.) For example, at Cosmopolitan College, the highest proportion of black students, 39 percent, were majoring in the social and behavioral sciences, with psychology, sociology, and political science the most popular. One-third of the blacks are in professional programs, particularly education and business administration. The remainder, 27 percent, was equally divided between the humanities and the physical and biological sciences and mathematics.

Although psychology, sociology, political science, education, and business administration are considered by many blacks to be

---

*A majority of white students have a similar orientation. However, only 55 to 60 percent of all white students, compared with the 70 to 75 percent of blacks, feel this is a very important goal of a college education.

TABLE 1

Academic Majors of Black and White Students at
an Upstate New York College, 1969-70
(in percent)

Field of Study	Black (N=67)	White (N=114)
Social and Behavioral Sciences:	38.8	25.4
Sociology	8.95	—
Political Science	7.5	6.1
Psychology	13.4	9.6
History	1.5	2.6
Economics	2.98	1.75
Anthropology	—	3.5
Area Studies	1.5	1.75
International Relations	1.5	—
Geography	1.5	—
Humanities:	13.4	20.2
Art	1.5	11.4
English	4.5	4.4
Languages	4.5	1.75
Religion	1.75	1.5
Philosophy	1.5	0.9
Physical Sciences and Mathematics:	13.4	11.4
Math	5.97	4.4
Biological Sciences	4.5	7.0
Chemical Sciences	2.98	—
Professional Studies:	34.4	43.0
Education	13.4	12.3
Journalism and TV-Radio	5.97	9.6
Business Administration	10.4	3.5
Speech and Drama	1.5	0.9
Home Economics	1.5	0.9
Nursing	—	0.9
Planning and Architecture	—	1.75
Public Administration	—	0.9
Social Work	—	0.9
Forestry	—	6.1
Engineering	1.5	5.3
Total	100.0	100.0

more relevant than other fields of study, some students assert that the ideas and information presented in all courses are useless and will be useless to them after graduation. This is the opinion of 55 percent of the black students included in our study. Blacks expect the social and behavioral sciences to deal with "real problems." In general, course content is described as real or relevant if it focuses upon the black experience. Some black students speak disparagingly of art courses that are concerned with the Greeks and Romans. Others are uninterested in international relations. Courses that impart information about American historical heroes such as George Washington are described by blacks as "brainwashing experiences."

Many blacks maintain that college courses ignore black problems and black life-styles. There are, for example, many complaints that black authors and black poets are ignored. Because black literature is seldom assigned, black students feel that they do not get an opportunity to learn things about themselves. Consequently, they believe that "black students don't learn much that would add . . . to their abilities." John, a second-year student who was born in a large city ghetto, described the need of black students to learn more about their people as "a necessary thing." Music was offered as one example of the avoidance of black life-styles. Some black students were critical of the lack of emphasis on jazz in music courses. They considered jazz to be a unique expression of the black experience and were disappointed that formal instruction in this music form was not available at most white colleges.

Students enrolled in courses in methods of education have had difficulty in securing experience as practice teachers in ghetto schools. Most arrangements for supervised classroom teaching at elementary and secondary school levels are made with affluent suburban school systems. Few blacks live in the communities surrounding these schools. For these and other reasons, the black students conclude that the education they are getting is geared toward whites and that their professors do not appreciate the black experience.

Only 45 percent of the black students (as compared to 65 percent of the white students) agree that they are able to fulfill themselves in their studies by pursuing their own interests. In addition, a majority of the blacks, 55 percent (as compared to only about one-third, or 37 percent, of the whites) have moderate to strong feelings that the ideas and information they are getting in college will not be useful after they leave school.

Black students accept the fact that some black people need to be trained as physicians, lawyers, and scientists. They do not set forth a program in Black Studies as a substitute for these disciplines. However, the process of labeling courses as "white-oriented" and the press for black awareness may create some identity conflicts for black students pursuing study in the sciences or professions. In a rap session on one campus, the black students said that black professionals play an important part in strengthening the black community. These students saw the Black Studies Program as a way of equipping the professionals with a state of mind that would enable them to go back into the community to serve the people.

Blacks believe that they ought to have the privilege of majoring in Black Studies if they wish to do so. Sarah, a third-year student, who majors in Television and Radio, said:

It's beautiful to be involved in the process of setting up Black Studies; but I'm a junior now and I'm really not going to benefit from it. . . . If I could come in as a freshman and there was a strong Black Studies Program here, I would never have majored in TV-Radio but in Black Studies." She indicates that she may major in Black Studies if she goes on for graduate education.

It is clear then that black students want Black Studies to fulfill a multitude of purposes. This may constitute the major difficulty in instituting such a program. It is proposed as a means of learning essential information, understanding the history of one's people, promoting black identity and solidarity, providing relevant academic experiences, straightening out oneself, and charting goals for the future. Thus, the program is expected to deal with the present, as well as the past, and personal, as well as public, concerns. It should convey a body of information, as well as induce a certain outlook on life or state of mind. It is fair to say that black students expect Black Studies to deal with both the prophetic and the pragmatic. As stated by Jim: "We are working on a life-time thing. With the creation of a Black Studies Program, I think we will have a black renaissance on a small scale right here. Creativity will bloom. Wow! Black Studies will just make things blossom—for me, anyway, and I think I speak for a lot of my brothers and sisters."

The Black Studies Program also would meet the criterion of relevancy alluded to so frequently by the black students. Relevancy is defined succinctly by Bill as "[anything] which has to do with me." As pointed out in another chapter, black students believe that anything having to do with their way of life is ignored or rejected by white teachers. Mary, a freshman, said that "the Black Studies Program

being pushed by the Black Student Union is one of the best things."
She talks about the Black Studies course in music literature at her
school and describes it as "a comfortable atmosphere [where] you're
learning about something you want to learn." This student also likes
her English class, because the professor uses a lot of "black books."
Several students, particularly those who have grown up in big northern
cities, state that they are bothered because they don't know much
about their background. The future and the past are united in the minds
of many black students. They believe that knowledge about the past
is an important prelude for the future. This statement is representative of the ideas of many. "We're going to have to know more about
our history to know who we are and where we are going."

A few blacks want a Black Studies Program because it will
benefit the whole school, including the white students. They see such
a program providing much-needed information for whites. One student
concludes that whites have cheated themselves educationally for hun-
dreds of years because of the exclusion of information about blacks.
Mike summarized his thoughts in this short phrase. "Whites need to
learn about us." Another student thought that whites not only would
learn about blacks but eventually would adopt a black perspective by
being exposed to Black Studies. "With the initiation of our methods
in the whole aspect of college life, the white school will learn from
it," said Clarence. He continued, "I believe, just like the white man
steals anything hip in our culture like music and dances, he will steal
our educational methods; he will steal our outlook on life. . . ."
Another student, Bob, speaks of the contribution that a Black Studies
Program could make to the entire school, but he is quick to point out
that the program first must consider the needs of blacks and that the
contribution must be made on the terms of blacks. Said he, "Ultimately, the Black Studies Program is for all kinds of students, but it
should be geared toward the blacks."

There is almost universal agreement among black students that
there should be a program of Black Studies at white colleges and they
also believe that the program should be controlled by blacks. There
is disagreement among blacks as to whether the program should be
available to whites. When Black Studies is looked upon as a way of
teaching whites about blacks, the black students tend to be against
establishing a separate program. But when the primary purpose is
to help blacks learn about themselves, and the teaching of whites is
secondary, then black students tend to prefer and even lobby for a
separate degree-granting program.

Most blacks included in this study, and particularly blacks

from stable working-class and middle-class families, preferred a
Black Studies Program with a sufficient number of courses to permit
a major or minor concentration. The few blacks who did not push for
a separate program feel that such a program might attract only a few
whites and that most white students would continue to take the traditional courses in which the black experience is omitted, ignored, or
distorted and would thus remain ignorant. These few blacks thought
that initially effort should be devoted to getting all courses revised
so that whites who are not likely to enroll in courses in a separate
Black Studies Program could learn why blacks are not going to take
any more of the "mess" they have put up with in the past. Even blacks
who are interested in a separate Black Studies Program share the
view that existing courses throughout the college need revising so that
they incorporate more accurately the black experience in America.
However, most blacks see this as a major effort, involving a great
hassle with a doubtful outcome.

Apparently, the majority of black students have given up on
attempts to educate whites by friendly persuasion. With the growing
interest in awareness and self-knowledge, they are more concerned
with developing separate academic structures where blacks can "do
their own thing." Moreover, they look upon a degree-granting Department of Black Studies as a power base in the academic community,
from which they can neogtiate with strength. With a separate department, it would be easier to get the courses and faculty they desire.

Both political power interests and academic concerns are joined
in proposals for Black Studies. For this reason, most black students
no longer care to cajole or persuade whites to include appropriate
materials about blacks in white-controlled courses. They have turned
their attention to educating themselves in a structure over which they
have some control. The overwhelming call for a separate Black
Studies Department is best understood as a manifestation of the growing
movement for self-determination. Thus, the decision of whether or
not to establish a Black Studies Department no longer can be limited
to only subject-matter considerations.

Black students believe that courses in Black Studies ought to
be taught by black professors, although they will accept a few white
teachers if they clearly are a minority of the teaching faculty in the
program. However, blacks stipulate that the few white instructors
in Black Studies programs must be "extra qualified." The following
black students discuss their preferences for black or white teachers
in Black Studies programs. These preferences are presented because
they are typical of the responses of other blacks when asked to comment
upon racial preference of teachers.

Ben: "Only blacks should teach [Black Studies] courses because there are things one can't get out of books."

Jane: "I would like to see a black person teaching the [Black Studies] course; but if there was a white person who was exceptionally qualified—but I would rather go out and look for a black person to fill the position first."

Sandra: "I think that only blacks should teach these [Black Studies] courses because when you teach about black people, only blacks can relate their experiences to the person being taught."

Marsha: "Black professors should be gotten to teach black courses whenever possible because with white professors there would be a problem with communication. If a white professor is extra qualified to teach a black course, we should keep a close eye on him and be extra critical of what he is saying."

Louis: "There should be an all-black or almost an all-black faculty in the Black Studies Department."

Dennis: "A Black Studies Department should be established at this school and run by and for blacks. Power must be in the hands of the people who are directly concerned."

Allen: "As far as faculty go [for the Black Studies Program], I would say vie for all the black faculty you can; and then when you run out of qualified black people, go to extra, extra qualified whites."

Cheryl: "Only black professors should teach these courses because they can relate to the course better: there's nothing like being black to deal with a black problem."

By and large, the students reported what they thought they would and would not like. Black students insist that experience with blacks rather than knowledge of blacks is the important quality for teachers of Black Studies. Using experience as a major criterion, black students can rule out the employment of whites until available black teachers have been considered; few whites in this segregated society have participated meaningfully in the black experience. These students feel that no matter how concerned, sympathetic, and knowledgable, whites must necessarily view the black experience from the outside. In this instance, intellectual and economic concerns are joined in the

statement of the criterion of teachers of Black Studies. By insisting
that professors in Black Studies have authentic experiences in the
black community, employment opportunities for the Black Studies
faculty is limited largely to blacks.

These preferences also reveal important themes in the black
experience. Apparently, blacks must accept a person first before
they can accept his or her ideas. Race has long been an impediment
to personal acceptance in American society, which is here manifested
in the rejection of whites by blacks. Whites, whom blacks now personally reject, they also reject professionally. One should be re-
minded that the prejudicial attitudes of blacks toward whites revealed
in this study are similar to the prejudicial attitude of whites toward
blacks revealed in other studies. In fact, the often-repeated statement
that any white who teaches in a Black Studies Program must be extra
qualified is a duplication of the requirement laid down for black teachers
by white colleges a decade or so ago.

Black Studies is a bona fide academic program and deals with
valid educational concerns. Black Studies also is a political instrument
through which power relationships between blacks and whites are balanced on white college campuses. Black Studies is a means for employment for black professors at white institutions. Black Studies
is a manifestation of the movement for self-determination. Black
Studies is all of this—a complex and confounding program.

CHAPTER

5

BLACK STUDENTS
AND
WHITE TEACHERS:
A LACK
OF TRUST

"Trust"—that's the main word, "said a group of blacks. "Black students need someone they can trust." Probably more significant than anything else in the educational process is the relationship between students and teachers, but black students do not trust their teachers. Black students charge that whites ignore the black experience. White teachers often fall short of fulfilling the expectations of blacks.

Black and white students have similar expectations about student rights and similar feelings about the extent to which these rights are respected and assured by the college. By and large, the students say that the colleges included in our study do not infringe upon their basic civil rights, such as due process, freedom of speech, freedom to assemble, freedom to petition about grievances, and freedom of press, as seen in Table 2.

While most of the black and white students felt that they had opportunities to be heard about curriculum, tuition, and other aspects of student life, a substantial minority (approximately one-third) felt there were little or no channels of communication. A similar proportion of students was critical of the due process afforded them and the degree of student representation on committees, such as those concerned with extracurricular activities. Of the blacks, 50 percent, compared to only 25 percent of the whites, felt that there was not equal access to scholarships. (The whole issue of financial aid will be discussed in a later chapter.)

We found that most students talk about the faculty a great deal outside class, but their actual contact with faculty members in settings other than the classroom is relatively low. Some 40 to 45 percent

TABLE 2

Student Rights—Extent of Effective Assurance on Four Upstate New York College Campuses, 1969-70 (percent)

Student Rights	Extent to Which Right is Effectively Assured on the Campus							
	Completely		As a General Rule		Very Little or None		Number	
	Black	White	Black	White	Black	White	Black	White
Student Self-Government by Representatives Freely Elected	19.0	19.8	59.5	60.4	21.5	19.8	163	202
Petitioning of Faculty and Administration with Respect to Curriculum, Tuition, and Other Conditions of Student Life	11.7	19.7	54.3	49.8	34.0	30.5	162	203
Due Process, Including Fair Notice, Counsel, and Specification of Charges in Cases of Suspension and Expulsion	14.7	17.2	55.1	54.7	30.1	28.1	156	203
Representation on Appropriate Faculty-Student or Administrative-Student Committees Concerned with Extra-curricular Activities	11.1	13.9	50.0	56.7	38.9	29.4	162	201
Freedom To Hear Outside Speakers on Any Subject Without Regard to Unpopularity of the Speaker	21.0	39.8	55.6	47.3	23.5	12.9	162	201

Freedom To Form Associations for Any Lawful Purpose and To Affiliate These with National Organizations, Including Political Organization, Provided that These Are Not Proscribed by Law	20.5	37.8	58.4	51.2	21.1	10.9	161	201
Freedom To Employ Facilities of the Institution, Such as Rooms and Bulletin Boards	29.8	37.9	48.4	51.7	21.7	10.3	161	203
Freedom To Choose Faculty Advisors for Student Groups Without Interference	22.5	14.5	50.6	67.5	26.9	18.0	160	200
Freedom of Press, Such as Student Newspapers and Magazines, with Free Access to Staff of Publications and with Adequate Provisions in case of Monopoly for the Expression of the Minority View	21.0	24.4	58.0	55.7	21.0	19.9	157	201
Freedom of Criticism, by Students, of Faculty or Administration	20.8	26.9	54.1	52.2	25.2	20.9	159	201
Freedom of Off-Campus Activity, Subject to Law or Community Standards of Taste; in Particular, Freedom To Engage in Political Activity with Minority Groups	26.4	44.0	47.9	46.5	25.8	9.5	163	200
Equal Access to Admissions, Scholarships, or Other Aid and to All Recognized Activities, Without Discrimination on Account of Race, Creed, or National Origins	13.0	28.6	36.4	46.8	50.6	24.6	162	203

of the students never conferred with a teacher during the course of a
semester. Of all students, 66.6 percent say that counseling and
guidance assistance is impersonal and insufficient, and 75 percent
feel that they get little, if any, help from faculty members and advisors.
The proportion of black and white students voicing these complaints
is similar.

The quality of the relationship between teachers and students
also tends to differ for blacks and whites. Indicators of the quality of
the relationship are the kinds of problems with which students turn
to teachers for assistance, the kinds of responses that teachers make,
and the perceptions of these responses by students.

The proportion of white students who would turn to their teachers
for positive academic guidance, such as registering, choosing classes
or instructors, buying books, and so on, is always larger than the
proportion of black students. For example, the 42 percent of white
students who say that they seek advice from faculty members about
choosing classes or instructors is more than twice as great as the 16
percent of black students who approach faculty members for this kind
of assistance. Similar ratios are found between blacks and whites
for other matters of academic guidance.

Probably one of the greatest differentiators between black and
white students with reference to their instructors, as we have noted,
is the lack of trust that black students have in white teachers. This
is indicated by the fact that only 36 percent of the black students
believe that the teacher is the appropriate person with whom to
register a complaint about an academic problem like grades, compared
with a majority (59 percent) of the white students. In fact, black
students tend to turn to the dean and other administrative personnel
to register a complaint about grades as often as they would turn
directly to the teacher. (This fact may be an indication, too, of a
differential feeling that blacks have about teachers, compared with
administrators—an issue which will be discussed later.) The proportion of whites who would take up the issue of grading with the teacher
first is twice as great as the proportion who would be inclined to go
to the dean. These data strongly suggest then that black students at
white colleges are less trusting of, and comfortable with, the faculty
than are white students.

A frequent complaint of black students is that white teachers
ignore them. Other complaints are that white teachers do not comprehend the black experience and discourage black students from
discussing and researching their racial heritage as an educational
exercise. A few complaints charge outright discrimination.

Gary, a student at a large college consisting of several thousand students, feels alienated and left out, as if he were "part of the factory." Giner, a freshman attending the same school, has had such limited contact with faculty that she confesses to not knowing what the teachers' attitudes really are toward black students. Hearsay is her only source of information. "I hear that some are racists and others are really great."

A male student, Winfred, at Metropolitan College, estimates that about one-fourth of the teachers ignore black students. The lamentations of one student recount an experience of professorial avoidance. Coleman reports:

> I tried to talk to him; he wouldn't talk to me. I went up to his office. He said he would meet me at 12:00 o'clock. I said, 'fine.' He never showed. I can't even get my paper back from him. He told me to go to the office to pick up my paper. He was in the cafeteria [one day] and was rapping to these white kids, telling them about their assignment. Why didn't he come and sit down at my table and explain what this story was about? . . . Then he goes into class and says 'blah, blah, blah,' and so forth. Well sure, these white kids know all about it because they heard about it ahead of time.

Ronald tells how a woman teacher walked away from him when he approached her for help and would not stop and acknowledge his presence until he swore at her. These experiences of disregard, avoidance, or refusal to take notice of blacks by whites are interpreted by some students as due to lack of sympathy. In the words of Morris: "I think the white teachers do not sympathize with the black students or do not try to help them if they are having trouble or problems with . . . one or two subjects. They tend to overlook them and tell them to get it the best way they can."

Many students believe that the faculty and administration try to pacify black students rather than respond to their demands and needs. As Joseph puts it, "They use a lot of trickery." Others interpret any evasive action as "conspiracy." Lack of trust in white colleges was clearly revealed in these remarks of George, who accuses the administration of Little Village College of "recruiting blacks indiscriminately," so that the ones of lesser ability would fail, and then the special program for the recruitment of black students could be declared unsuccessful. When the actions of faculty are seen to work in the black students' favor, such as giving them a strong benefit of the doubt, white faculty are viewed by the blacks as hypocritical and

patronizing. Ben sums up the collective sentiment of his black colleagues this way: "What we need is for people to be honest with us."
Johnny said that the teachers in his school were unaware of the problems and responsibilities of black students and refused to relate to
the black experience. He said:

> It's like this, man. I am black and I want to write about
> black people. When I do this, I learn more about my
> people and also I can tell it like it is. The professor
> doesn't understand, nor can he dig how we feel. He is
> against black kids writing about black people. . . .
> I write about black people anyway. My grade on the
> paper might not be very good; but that will not stop
> me. I might get it put to me in the end when final
> marks come around, but, like, that's okay, too.

Phyllis, a third-year student studying at Cosmopolitan College,
faults the administration for being "ignorant of black needs and attitudes."

    In a rap session of black students on campus, one attributed
the low mark that a teacher gave him on a composition as due to the
fact that the paper was "written from a black perspective," which the
student claims the professor "couldn't understand." Cliff, a senior
political science major at Small City College, described his teachers
as "educated fools." He said that "so many of them are not used to
the environments and conditions that black people have had to live
through," and, therefore, find it difficult, if not impossible, to
understand blacks. He bemoaned the fact that white teachers tend to
think that a perspective which is different from their own is wrong.
A black freshman tried to explain the lack of understanding of the
black experience by white teachers this way:

> Like I dig jazz. That's my whole life. . . . Here, they
> don't do what I dig. In fact, I went to my music professor
> and I told him my thing. He said he liked it, but I guess
> he didn't like it enough, 'cause he never mentioned it in
> class. . . . There's a whole span of jazz that develops
> from blues. It's from here that the rhythm and blues
> stuff comes; rock originates from here. But they don't
> talk about it [at this school].

    Oscar also talked about another music-related incident. "The
English teacher assigned students [phonograph] records to write
about, all white rock and roll artists. When confronted as to why no

black records were assigned, the teacher said, 'I don't know any
black records. I have never heard any.'" And so the story goes—
blacks distrusting whites and believing that whites are disinterested
in black customs and culture. Whether or not whites are as disinterested as blacks assert cannot be determined fully from the data at
hand. However, it is clear that many blacks tend to perceive and
believe whites to be thoroughly disinterested in the black experience.
Perceptions and beliefs are critically important in determining black
reactions to white college campuses, especially their reactions to
teachers and members of the college administration. Beliefs tend to
father reality and, therefore, affect social relationships.

These opinions, which express the idea that the college faculties
are biased and inflexible in regard to black students, are supported
by our data collected in the survey. The percent of black students
responses to questions on the faculty are shown in Table 3. These
data indicate that a lower proportion of black students, compared to
white students, feel that faculty are willing to talk with students,
maintain receptiveness to new ideas, or allow students to pursue their
individual interests. Further, data presented in Table 3 indicate
that a large proportion of black students do not feel that faculty evaluate
their work fairly.

Instances of deliberate discrimination are not mentioned often.
There were a few reported incidents, however, such as the one
presented by Charlene, who felt that her speech teacher always found
something wrong with her presentation whenever it had anything to do
with the black experience, or the one presented by Dave, who felt
that one of his teachers ganged up with the white students against him
whenever the classroom discussion drifted to the subject of race.
Whether these incidents are manifestations of actual discrimination
or descriptions of supersensitivity of those involved cannot be determined. Despite recent recruitment campaigns, we found most blacks
believe that the teachers and administrators do not welcome them.
Many see themselves merely as being tolerated as "token blacks."

Some blacks have had more pleasant experiences at these schools
and are more positive about their campus community. A few students
even report that the administration in many instances appears to be
leaning over backwards to give blacks the benefit of the doubt. On
one campus, for example, a black student believed the office of the
dean to be somewhat more lenient with blacks than with whites in
calling in students for conferences about cutting classes. Praise
frequently was given to the members of the administration who made
it possible for blacks to have their own facilities, such as a separate

TABLE 3

Opinions of Black and White Students About Faculty at
Four Upstate New York Colleges, 1969-70
(percent)

Students Agree that . . .	Black		White	
In general Faculty Are Willing To Talk with Students About Their Ideas[a]	78.8	(N=165)	92.2	(N=205)
Generally Faculty are Receptive to Students' New Ideas[b]	74.7	"	81.3	"
Professors Try To Provoke Arguments and Discussions in Class, the Livelier the Better[b]	48.8	"	48.5	"
Students in This School Are Allowed To Pursue Their Individual Interests in Their Work[b]	44.5	"	65.4	"
Teamwork and Cooperation Are Strongly Emphasized[b]	40.5	"	43.0	"
Evaluation of Classroom Work by Faculty Is Conducted in a Fair Manner[a]	55.8	(N=163)	73.2	(N=201)
The Procedures in Approaching Most of the Student's Work Are Defined for Him[a]	54.6	"	38.3	"
Faculty Expect All Students To Conform to a Fairly Standardized Level of Performance[a]	86.5	"	73.8	"
Rigidly Adhered to, Standardized Procedures Are Employed in Evaluating Our Work	32.5	"	45.4	"

[a]This includes "willing" and "somewhat willing" responses.
[b]This includes "strongly agree" and "agree" responses.

house, a special lounge, or a section of a dormitory. While several students described faculty members as helpful, members of the administration gathered the most compliments from the black students. They tended to be characterized as "cooperative," or "fair," or "understanding," or "easy to approach" by those students who were favorably disposed toward administrative responses. The black students who have had good experiences with members of the college administration expressed regret that they tend not to come into contact with officials unless there is a confrontation.

Earlier, we mentioned that individual black students are as likely to go to the dean as to a faculty member to register complaints about academic problems and that this action is unlike the behavior of white students, who are more inclined to deal directly with their professors. Presumably, the blacks expect to receive more understanding from administrative officers and less cooperation from the faculty. At one institution, the black students described the administration as "liberal: and the faculty as 'conservative.' " . . . The hard core faculty members do not want to have a damn thing to do with students. . . . They don't want students on their damn committees. And when the shit comes down, the teachers don't want anything to do with black students at all or any of their problems."

While black students tend to have more confidence in white administrators than in white faculty members, their confidence is not overwhelming. Indeed, their faith in the administration is shaky. For example, nearly one out of every two black students believes that the administration is intolerant of student protests and suggestions for changing the school. Of the black students, 50 percent give the administration the benefit of the doubt and 50 percent do not.

This means that on white college campuses, black advisors and faculty are essential if black students are to have any confidence in the operation of the institution. The black advisor has been varyingly described as "someone you can talk to," "a source of information," "really concerned," "someone with whom you can identify," and "someone who can ease the pain a little bit." The important counseling function that a black advisor performs on a white college campus is perhaps described by Henry:

[The black advisor] has brought the black community at this school together. I was excited when we heard that [a black advisor] was coming, because this was a start. I usually talk to [the black advisor] twice a week. [The advisor] shows initiative and passes on the initiative to us.

It is like having a black person looking over you, telling
you where it's at. If you don't study or if you goof off,
[the advisor] tells you that you're not acting like a black
man. If teachers have any problems or questions, they
call [the black advisor] also, so [the advisor] is serving
both ways. [The black advisor] gives me about 75 percent
of my ideas, and many times compliments those I come
up with. [The black advisor] tells me how to present
demands to the administration and faculty because, man,
I don't know how to present demands to anyone. I don't
know how to ask the Student Council for $100 to bring
back a black rock group to campus. They [the Student
Council members] use all that parliamentary procedure.
[The black advisor] tells me how to [draft and] present
[my proposal] and I'll write it up. Until I learn how to
do it, I'll be dependent on [the black advisor]. I couldn't
do without [the black advisor] at all. . . .

This magnificant testimony about the role and function of a black
advisor on a white college campus is significant. It explains why a
higher proportion of black students are more inclined to go to the
black advisor rather than to white faculty members for help with
strictly academic matters, such as registration and the choosing of
classes and instructors. Slightly more than one-third of the black
students in the colleges in our study turned to the black advisor for
assistance in these matters, compared with approximately one-sixth
who turned to white faculty members for academic advice. For extracurricular activities, such as finding a job around the campus, again
the black students are more inclined to consult the black advisor than
to approach a white administrator. In fact, 53 percent of the black
students reported that they would go to the black advisor for help in
finding a job, compared with 15 percent who thought the office of the
dean was a more appropriate place to find employment assistance.

Not only do black students express an overwhelming need for
black advisors, they also press for more black faculty. They feel
the need for black faculty members to teach courses that focus on
the black experience. Our study obtained indications of the expectation
that black students hold for black faculty members beyond their teaching
functions. Their expectations are unique and different from expectations in the student body at large. These expectations are held by a
majority of the black students.

First, black students believe that black faculty members should
place loyalty to the race above loyalty to the college. This point of

view was clearly articulated when the black students indicated that they believed black faculty should bypass channels in order to get something done or should break school rules when in the interest of blacks.

While most black students realized that black faculty members ought to work with the entire student body, at least four out of every ten would prefer that blacks work only with blacks. This expectation held by a minority (nevertheless, a sizable one) of the black students probably is at variance with the views of the student body at large more than any other expectation for black faculty members. Approximately 90 percent of the white students believe that black faculty members should work with all students. The expectations of black students for black faculty constitute a potential source of stress, which could result in strained relationships between black faculty and white members of the campus community. The double loyalties that the black faculty member is expected to hold—loyalty to the race and its members and loyalty to the college and its constituents—could come into conflict with each other.

Better communication between black students and the teachers and administrators at white schools might help alleviate some of the problems. However, it is well known that facts alone are insufficient in changing attitudes, perceptions, and beliefs. If the feelings of distrust and lack of confidence should crystalize among black students so much that they become cynical, it would be difficult for white faculty members and administrators to change such a belief system of blacks simply by becoming sympathetic and concerned. Because black students on many white college campuses are rapidly approaching a state of cynicism, black administrators and faculty are essential. They may function as a channel of credibility between the black students and the predominantly white institution. It is possible that black students will develop confidence and trust in white colleges and in their white colleagues only if they can develop confidence and trust in some of the people attached to these institutions. Although there is no guarantee, black administrators and faculty are the most likely candidates to encourage such trust on the part of black students.

Of course, it is important to recognize the complexity of the problem and the elusiveness of a simple solution. While black faculty and administrators may help to reconcile black students and white institutions by bridging credibility and confidence gaps, the conflicting expectations and demands placed upon these persons by black and white members of the college community could contribute to much strain and ultimately to their undoing. The status and roles of black faculty and administrators in white colleges are a classic example of cross pressures and structural strains in a social system. Black administrators are likely to experience these pressures and strains due to their position in the organizational structure of a school, especially if their formal responsibilities involve advising black members of the student body at the same time they are expected to advise white members of the faculty and administration.

6

A NEW
AND AMBIGUOUS ROLE:
THE BLACK ADVISOR
ON THE
WHITE COLLEGE CAMPUS

Our impression is that possibly more confusion surrounds the role of the black advisor than that of any other role in white colleges. The prestige, power, and responsibilities of the black advisor are a formal set of issues lacking clarification and consensus. Informal sources of difficulty emerge from variations in perceptions and expectations with respect to the role of a black advisor. If roles are a function of the definition of the situation by the actor and his associates, then it is fair to say that the role of the black advisor is potentially laden with great conflict. In spite of its difficulties, the black advisor role is an exciting one, because it is situated at a point of intersection between faculty, students, and administration. It is a demanding role, permitting its incumbent few false moves and almost no mistakes. So much depends on its effectiveness. Failure could damage a fragile institution.

The position of black advisor may also be complicated by the fact that he or she must be approved by the black students. This is in contrast to the usual procedure for other college counselors. The white counselor is, in most cases, an administrative appointee, with fairly explicit responsibilities; moreover, he or she is directly accountable to higher officers in the administration. The black advisor, although appointed by the administration, is also subjected to the demands of black students, whose confidence he must have in order to function effectively.

The ambiguity of the black advisor role was most clearly seen in the different ways in which it had been structured into the school. Most black advisors had dual roles—advisor-administrator or advisor-teacher. One advisor had assigned responsibilities limited to counseling and, as he was not expected to perform any teaching or administrative functions, appeared to have greater access to, and more regularized contact with, high administrative officials on campus. While it may be an asset to tie on the black advisor role to an administrative or teaching role that is more clearly understood in the college community, the additional role may be a liability. For example, one black advisor who also taught discovered that black students lumped his course in with the others that were declared irrelevant for the black experience.

The black advisor, as used in this study, is a generic term that refers to the highest administrative officer for black affairs on each campus. The additional information on the black advisor's perceptions were obtained by interviews conducted by brown and white full-time faculty members—one a sociologist and the other an anthropologist. A limitation of our study is that information was not obtained about the expectations of white faculty and administration for the black advisor to compare with the black advisor's own definition of his role and the definitions of black students.

The black advisors were recruited in several different ways. Although the various individuals have positions located at different places in the administrative hierarchy, all four were appointed by the administration with little, if any, advice from the faculty. In some instances, the position was created to fulfill the requirements of a specially funded program. Two of the black advisors were sought to fill the positions that were created as a consequence of black students' demands. One advisor was a member of the faculty before assuming the new responsibility. The other three black advisors were specially recruited outside the schools. On two campuses, black advisors were the only blacks to hold faculty or administrative positions.

Black advisors saw their new roles in several ways. The definition of the role ranged all the way from helping with the problems of individuals to attempting to bring about institutional change. Some also found themselves teaching students to recognize institutionalized racism, to resist oppression, and to discover their identity. Educating white faculty and administration about the way of life and problems of minority group members was high on the agenda of one advisor; his view was that the opportunity system was blocked on campus for black students due to white racism. Another advisor interpreted his role as being basically that of an intercessor, cajoling the system into responding to the needs of black students, explaining to the students the complexities of the system, and helping them to maneuver within it better. Another advisor almost ignored the system within which students operated, took a personal approach, and concentrated on helping students individually. Thus, there is a distinct difference between methods of working with students.

Most advisors believed that they could not speak for the black students and, therefore, avoided giving this appearance. Some thought, however, that they should use their official and sometimes personal contacts with the administration to obtain opportunities for the black students that the students themselves were unable to obtain.

The campus location of the black advisor's office seemed to be an unresolved issue. Black advisors were housed in a dormitory, an administration building, and in an ethnic cultural center. Should the black advisor be housed in the administration building, so that, through frequent contact with other administrators, he or she might further the cause of blacks on campus? Or should the advisor be housed in a separate facility, where more frequent contacts might be established with blacks and other minority groups as a way of better understanding their concerns? No adequate answer was provided for these persisting questions. An advisor in the administration building thought that he would be more effective were he located in a separate cultural center. On the other hand, a black advisor in a separate cultural center felt the need for more frequent and regularized contacts with other administrative officers. Whether or not location of an office in or outside the administration building contributed to more or less power, authority, and effectiveness could not be determined from the data available for this analysis.

Of course, factors other than office ecology may play an important role in facilitating or hindering the program of the black advisor. All of the advisor positions have been newly created because of the introduction of increased numbers of black students on white college campuses. Appointments are made at different levels in the bureaucratic hierarchy of colleges. The positions ranged from that of a counselor (in the conventional sense) to that of a high policy-making administrative position.

Recognizing that we cannot generalize on the basis of interviews with four black advisors, an overview of these data suggest some hypotheses that might be explored in future research. It should be determined whether or not locating the black advisor in the upper region of the university administrative hierarchy contributes to or impedes innovative activity, such as the introduction of Black Studies and other new programs. Further study is needed to determine whether or not the black advisor is more helpful to students personally if he or she is limited to counseling or has a combined teaching and counseling role.

We also determined the expectations of black students for black advisors. Our purpose was to learn if there was congruence or divergence in student and advisor expectations regarding the black advisor role. These data are reported in Table 4. Because the students were asked to indicate their expectations for black faculty as well as black advisors, it cannot be determined from these data what differences in expectations, if any, students held for black advisors alone.

Basically, black students expected black advisors to be a resource but not to attempt to speak for them. They were adamant in rejecting the idea that black faculty and advisors should be free to make decisions about black students without consulting them. And two-thirds said they strongly believed that black faculty members and advisors should keep black students informed about campus happenings. This indicates the importance of the black faculty and advisor as communication links on campus.

Black students accepted the intercessory function of black faculty members and advisors with other school officials. An overwhelming majority (87 percent) expected people filling these roles to negotiate with administration and faculty on behalf of specific black students experiencing difficulties. Presumably, this expectation was due to a perceived imbalance in power, with students having less power. Where the power relationships were more equal, such as between black and white students, some black students were prepared to fight their own battles. There was indecision about whether black faculty and advisors should mediate between black and white students; 56 percent said they should, and 44 percent said they should not. However, the fact that a majority of the black students expected some advice and support from black faculty members and advisors, even in their relationships with other students, indicated that black students experienced a considerable amount of anxiety and uncertainty on white college campuses.

The expressed need to lean on someone for advice and assistance should not be misinterpreted as a call for special favors. Black students tended to see black teachers and advisors as members of the faculty and administration and they more or less expected the incumbents to honor the requirements of these roles. But there was a great amount of uncertainty as to whether the primary loyalty of the advisor should be to the race or to the institution, as mentioned in an earlier chapter.

TABLE 4

Black Student Expectations of Black Faculty and Advisors at Four
Upstate New York Colleges, 1969-70
(percent)

Black Faculty Members and Counselors Should . . .	Strongly Expect and Expect Most of the Time	Do Not Expect or Does Not Matter
Come up with New Ideas for Handling the Problems of Black students on This Campus	84.5 (160)	15.5
Spend Some Time Other Than During the Workday with Black Students	77.8	22.2
Work More with All (Black and White) Students on the Campus	58.7	41.3
Serve as a Mediator Between Black Students and Other Students	55.6	44.4
Help To Organize Black Student Activities and Organizations	81.9	18.1
Work Only with Black Students	40.1	59.9
Consult More Closely with Black Students Before Making any Decisions Affecting Them	96.9	3.1
Keep Black Students Informed on What Is Happening Around the School	89.5	10.5
Break Official School Rules When It Is in the Interest of Black Students	56.3	43.7
Bypass Official Channels When Something Has To Be Done	65.0	35.0
Carry Out Administrative Rules, Even if They Might Think Them Unsound	20.5	79.5
Withhold Information from Administrators or Faculty that Might Put a Black Student in a Bad Light	46.9	53.1
Tell Higher-Ups His Frank Position, Even if It Might Jeopardize His Position	76.4	23.6
Communicate with Other Faculty About Problems that a Particular Black Student May Be Having	86.7	13.3
Serve as Mediator Between Black Students and the School Administrators	85.7	14.3

Some attitudes and values of the black students transcended racial considerations: 75 percent believed that one should speak one's opinion even if it placed one's job in jeopardy, and 80 percent believed that a teacher or advisor should not be expected to carry out administrative regulations when in his judgment he believed them to be unsound.

Finally, the responses suggested that most black students were uncertain about whether they should jealously hoard the time and talents of black faculty members and advisors: 40 percent expected these black adults on campus to work with blacks most of the time or all of the time, but 60 percent did not. This 40-60 split is a rather close division, suggesting a lack of consensus.

A number of reasons could be stated to explain why some black students prefer that black teachers and advisors work only with blacks—some psychological and some educational. As Catherine said, "Blacks are more comfortable with blacks"; black students can move faster in learning something about themselves when they and the black faculty are not hung up trying to educate whites. Also, there are political reasons why some black students prefer that black teachers and advisors work only with blacks. Harry Edwards informs us that black students are increasingly demanding some decision-making power in determining who should be hired.* It is he who appoints the piper, as well as he who pays the piper, who calls the tune. Black students have recognized this revision in the old adage and are moving quickly to implement it with reference to black teachers and advisors on campus. Those who recommend appointments are especially powerful if they have the power of recall.

While black students were undecided (collectively) about whether black teachers and advisors should be available to the entire student body, three of the four black advisors said they worked with other students as well as blacks. They said this was an appropriate extension of the black advisor role. Specifically mentioned was help given to other minority group members, such as Puerto Ricans and American Indians. Two of the advisors said they also worked with a few white students who dropped by their offices from time to time.

Before considering discrepancies, if any, in the definition of the black advisor role by the students and by the incumbents, a brief

----

*Harry Edwards, Black Students (New York: The Free Press, 1970), p. 70.

statement should be made about how the administration and faculty view this role. As mentioned earlier, no systematic information was collected from these members of the campus community. We have available for analysis then, only the advisors' impressions of the whites in the administration and faculty. One advisor reported having weekly meetings with the college president and said, "the administrators appear willing" to facilitate ways of meeting the needs of black students. However, she noted a serious lack of coordination between faculty and administration. The implication was that faculty were not as "willing." Another advisor, when questioned about his role, responded, "It would probably be more appropriate to ask the administration what they think I should be doing." The statement implied that he did not have a clear understanding of the administration's expectations for the black advisor role. When comparing the administration with the faculty, this same advisor felt that his main problem had come from the faculty. A third advisor said: "I can go to anyone in the administration at any time and get a hearing. I have many more problems with the faculty than with administrators. The faculty creates stumbling blocks and is not in tune with what is needed." A fourth advisor put it this way: "The faculty, they don't understand. A lot of them think there is some special handout for blacks. [The dean] is very good. He has had experience, doesn't get all hung-up in all that administration bullshit." What is clear from these statements is that all is not well between faculty members and black advisors and that black advisors have a better working relationship with the administrators.

In general, we found that most black advisors on white college campuses had to define their own roles, with little help from the administrators, with some hindrance from the faculty, and, oftentimes, with indifference on the part of students. Among advisors, however, some convergence in role definition was beginning to appear. Black advisors in at least three of the four colleges saw themselves as resource persons for troubled black youth. Black students as well as the advisor felt that he or she ought to be available for personal and academic assistance. Most black advisors were willing to serve as security blankets for troubled black students, and some lamented the fact that their skills were not sufficiently developed to more effectively fulfill this function. Others felt that they were too deeply involved in campus affairs to give as much time to supportive counseling as needed. The colleges were criticized for not hiring enough advisors to do a better job of personal counseling.

The black advisors saw the need to intervene directly in the policy-making of the educational system to make it a more satisfying

experience for black students. Black advisors were seriously concerned about the curriculum, supportive and remedial services, the
hiring of more black teachers, student recruitment, arrangements
for financial assistance, and so on. They often had to negotiate directly
with the administration and the faculty about many of these issues.
It is in performing these functions that black advisors and black students may conflict with each other, due to the black students' growing
concern about anyone speaking for them without authorization. Actually, black students can pull the rug out from under black advisors
at any time if they declare that they no longer have confidence in them.
In the light of our analyses, one can understand how the black advisor's role can become complicated, almost to the point of becoming
unbearable, if the administration and the faculty expect him to be
beholden to them while black students insist he serve as their representative and interpreter.

    In due time, the black advisor role probably will emerge with
a well-defined set of expectations of what is required, permitted, or
prohibited of one who fills this role in the academic community.
Eventually, the black advisor position is likely to fractionate into two
separate functions. One function will focus on reorganizing the educational institution, including rooting out expressions of racism in
the construction of the curriculum, in the recruitment of students,
and in the assignments of faculty and other significant personnel in
the academic enterprise. The other function will focus on personal
and supportive services to individual black students.

    The individual and the institution are intertwined and complement
each other, so that it is hard to deal with one without considering the
other. The amount of time required of the advisor to deal with the
multitude of problems presented by either the institution or the individual is so overwhelming that usually one or the other gets slighted.
Some advisors are more talented in dealing with institutional arrangements, while others are more effective when assisting individuals.
The separation of these two functions will make for less frustration
among black advisors, who are now struggling to fill both of these
functions with little understanding of why their role is so exhausting.

    The ambiguities and conflicts in the black advisor role are
likely to continue for the foreseeable future, largely because this role
has come into being during a great transitional period in the college
community. The balance of power between student body, faculty,
and administration has been upset, and a redistribution is in process.
Existing authority structures are being challenged on all fronts, and
it is not yet clear what the new pattern of structure for the governance

of the college will be. Because it is difficult to determine exactly what power reposes in each campus constituency, it is difficult to predict how and in favor of which group—students, faculty, administration—black advisors will resolve their role conflict. The group that is perceived as having power one day may not be so perceived another day in a rapidly changing system. Thus, the black advisor tends to be cautious and cagey.

RECRUITMENT
AND
FINANCIAL AID

At our four institutions, the enrollment of black students is less than 2 percent. Each school is making a major effort to increase the number of blacks on campus, but the enlarged black student population in the freshman class, compared with the other classes, is evidence of the recency of this recruitment drive.

A method of recruiting black students that appears to be successfully used by some of the schools we studied is the involvement of black students in the recruitment of new students. Gretchen, a freshman at Metropolitan College, is a member of a committee of black students who go to the local high schools to talk with black graduating seniors about continuing their education. In these recruitment missions, specific information about the college faculty, scholarships, and other kinds of aid is shared. Also, they are told about the black organizations on campus that are available to black students. The Union of Black Collegians and the Student Afro-American Society have been particularly helpful in recruiting black students. Several students in these organizations have been asked to take on recruitment assignments in their hometowns. One student said that her college had encouraged the black organizations to recruit "hard-core ghetto students" for the next semester. She was especially pleased about this. As stated by Glenn, who receives an EOG: "We recruit a lot of people. We're trying to recruit more kids. Whenever we go to a party or any place, we talk about [this college]. We hope to get 100 kids here next year." Presently, there are fewer than 40 black students on his college campus.

The black students are not pleased with the current number of blacks on any of the campuses included in our study. They believe

there should be more. They place the major responsibility for recruitment upon the administrative personnel, although they are willing
to participate in the recruitment process. The administration at most
white colleges is accused of not being sufficiently aggressive in the
recruitment of black students.

Even though they cooperate by participating in recruitment programs, many black students continue to be deeply suspicious of the
motives and intentions of the administrators and are quick to charge
admission officers with bad faith. Tom said: "We go home to our
high schools and tell them about Small City College and tell them to
write. They have, but they haven't gotten an answer. I guess the
administration can tell by where they live that they are blacks." A
middle-aged graduate student, Rosie Mae, enrolled in a small department in Cosmopolitan College, has been asked to be in charge of the
recruitment committee of her department. She believes that she has
been asked to assume this responsibility because she is the only black
student in that department. While she has accepted this responsibility,
she said, "I . . . feel that recruitment should be a paid position that
Cosmopolitan College should be in charge of." There is a hint in Rosie
Mae's remarks that she believes she is being exploited. Yet, she and
others who grumble from time to time are willing to participate in
recruitment because it offers the possibility of enlarging the black
student population on campus. Thus, the recruitment of black students
is a project in which the administration and blacks cooperate, despite
the one-sided or mutual suspicion that may exist. From a black
perspective, more blacks on campus means political power and an
enriched social life, even though it is also believed that the college
will use the enlarged black population on campus as evidence to deny
allegations of racism that have been lodged against many white institutions. Black students believe the white colleges they attend are
more interested in keeping their own skirts clean than in providing a
relevant education for blacks. The black students also believe the
public institutions are recruiting them mainly because they are required
to participate in specially funded programs for minority students. For
these reasons, the blacks insist that the colleges should do more than
recruit only a token number, which is what they suspect most institutions plan to do.

Indeed, the awkward way in which some of the schools have gone
about recruiting blacks when no black staff members were available
to help has contributed to the impressions mentioned above. This is
illustrated in the remarks of several black students in a rap session
at Little Village College:

Do you think the administration is hesitant to bring more blacks on campus?

Well. . . .

I think they have within the administration some kind of quota, quota, [you know, an] amount they gotta drag in—100 or 200 blacks.

Well, they realize now that they have to have so many black students on their campus. In other words we're token niggers on the campus.

．．．．．

This is really the reason they get black men on campus: 'Cause they have to have them.

．．．．．

What about the people that come? I mean, what type of person recruits the black people?

．．．．．

Well, Mr. Green; now they appointed him as a recruiter for black students because he headed a black regiment while serving in the war. So they figure: 'Well, he's had a little to do with black people, so maybe he'd be the best since he went through this.' This might sound funny but it's true.

Did you talk with Mr. Green before you came here?

Right! I did. Mr. Green came to my high school, you know. They came in the winter, you know. They were pretty friendly. But the way he put it—like he needed us for some reason beside education, you know. He was too quick— like, 'You can come. I'll live with you, too,' you know.

．．．．．

Did he say that?

Not in the same words. That's what the overall picture was. . . .

. . . . .

I got the same impression, man. I talked with him over the
phone. . . . My cousin goes here; he's a senior. He said,
'Call Mr. Green, man.' I called him and said, 'Mr. Green,
I'm interested in your college and from what [my cousin]
told me, it sounds like a pretty good deal. So I would like
very much to apply there and see if I could get in.' He said,
'Don't worry about that. You're in. You're automatically in.'

. . . . .

I went to see this guy that was the recruiter for two-year
colleges. And he told me to get my application and everything and send them to Little Village College. Now, this
[was] the end of July, almost the beginning of August. And
the second or third week in August, I was accepted.

. . . . .

Did they know you were black?

Hell, yeah! On the Education Opportunity Grant program?

You bet your life!

. . . . .

That's a shame, man. It's not a shame. But, you know,
just the system they got up here. . . .

That's the one generalization I get about Little Village
College. . . . They'll accept us just as long as we're black.
No matter how we're qualified. You know what I mean?
They'll put us in a program; they'll put us in a major, and
knowing we can't make it, but just putting us there because
we're black.

. . . . .

Knowing we can't make it!

. . . . .

So much money was appropriated last year for black students
and because Little Village College has so few. . . . So they

had to accept so many [but] not over [a certain] amount for this school. . . .

From the foregoing, it is clear that the relationship between black students and white colleges is characterized by deep-seated distrust by blacks, even when financial opportunities are provided by the schools. Because of this persisting feeling, it is most important that white colleges involve black staff in the recruitment and admissions process. Black students tend to believe that there is a greater chance black staff will be more interested in the welfare of the black individual.

Despite the awkwardness of recruiting officers, the previous remarks of the students demonstrate that visiting and talking directly with black students is a successful method of recruitment. Several students indicated that they came to a particular school because a representative personally approached them at their high school or elsewhere in their hometown community.

The utilization of black students is a very successful way of recruiting other black students. Black students are willing to participate in recruitment programs because of self-interest. This explains why some black students will invite other blacks to become members of a white college community that they admittedly distrust. It would be a grave mistake for whites to assume that the participation of blacks in student recruitment campaigns is a sign of school loyalty.

The high school counselor also may be an important agent in referring black students to white colleges. Of the black students, 25 percent said their high school counselor suggested a particular institution—in many instances, contacted the admissions office on behalf of the student and worked out special support arrangements. Nevertheless, approximately 75 percent of the black students made their way to college without the assistance of a counselor. The meaning of this fact is unclear, but it does suggest that the influence of the counselor is not pervasive.

A college must offer liberal financial aid if it is to recruit minority students. In his study of midwestern colleges, Warren W. Willingham discovered that 80 percent of the minority students needed financial aid. He further found that 13 percent of all freshmen in these schools, compared with 41 percent of the minority freshmen, needed full financial support.* Our study indicates that limited income created

---

*Warren W. Willingham, Admission of Minority Students in Midwestern Colleges (Evanston, Ill.: College Entrance Examination Board, 1970), p. 7.

similar problems for black students in upstate New York.   Comparative
data for blacks and whites are presented in Table 5.

Black students in white colleges come, as a rule, from families
with modest economic resources. This fact is demonstrated by the
data in Table 5. The median annual income for the fathers of black
students—approximately $8,000—is only two-thirds as large as the
median yearly income for the fathers of white students—about $12,000.

We found that about one out of every fifteen black students (6.5
percent) could be classified as extremely poor; the head of the household in such families received less than $3,000 a year. Also, there
were few very affluent black families. Only 5 or 6 percent of the black
students came from families in which the fathers had an annual income
of $20,000 or more. The picture among whites was different. At
least 25 percent of the white students had fathers who earned more
than $20,000 a year, and only one out of every twenty-seven (or 3.7
percent) were extremely poor.

Neither the income of white or black fathers is sufficient for the
skyrocketing costs of a college education. Dual employment of mother
and father often is required. Women worked in a majority of the black
and white households: 61 percent of the white mothers and 78 percent
of the black mothers. Looked at in another way, one might say the
proportion of mothers not in the labor force in households with college-
matriculating students is almost twice as great for white households
(39 percent), as compared with black households (22 percent).

Because of their disadvantaged circumstances, most of the black
students (nearly nine out of every ten, or 88 percent) believed that
scholarships especially designed for blacks should be set aside. Blacks
contend that it creates false hopes to open the doors of white colleges
but not to provide the necessary financial aid. On the other hand, a
majority of white students (70 percent) believe that no special scholarships should be reserved exclusively for blacks. The white students
did not volunteer any opinions on what adjustments they thought should
be made to compensate for the unequal financial circumstances of
black and white families. The belief of some whites that blacks are
receiving preferential treatment has been a bone of contention between
students in the two racial populations.

The economic resources of many black parents are too limited
to allow them to pay for a college education for their children while
maintaining the regular expenses of a household. Of the black students
enrolled in the four colleges, 63 percent were supported by sources

TABLE 5

Annual Income of Father for Black and White Students at Four
Upstate New York Colleges, 1969-70
(percent)

Annual Income in Dollars	Blacks (N=139)			Whites (N=190)		
	Male	Female	Total	Male	Female	Total
$ 3,000	5.9	7.1	6.5	4.5	2.6	3.7
$ 3,000-$ 5,000	13.2	7.1	10.1	5.4	5.1	5.3
$ 5,000-$ 7,500	26.5	28.6	27.2	15.3	11.5	13.7
$ 7,500-$10,000	27.9	22.9	25.2	21.6	15.4	19.5
$10,000-$20,000	20.6	28.6	25.2	32.5	34.7	33.1
$20,000-$30,000	4.4	0	2.2	12.6	11.5	12.1
$30,000 +	1.5	5.7	3.6	8.1	19.2	12.6
Total	100.0	100.0	100.0	100.0	100.0	100.0

other than their parents. Only 46 or 47 percent of the white students
said they were supported by nonfamily resources, as seen in Table 6.
A majority of the white college students (53.5 percent) received support from their parents, but this was the experience of only 38 percent
of the black students. Nearly two-thirds of the black students (63 percent) received financial aid from their schools, including direct grants
and compensation for work on campus. Approximately 22 percent of
the black students received assistance from sources not specified.
Were black students who received financial support from unspecified
sources other than parents added to those identified as receiving direct
support from their schools, the proportion of assisted students would
be similar to the 80 percent of minority students who required financial
aid reported in the midwestern colleges study.

The black students at white colleges come from a wide variety
of backgrounds. Among the professions represented by their parents
are farm laborers, construction workers, physicians, insurance agents,
telephone operators, case workers, barbers, beauticians, private
household workers, restaurant owners, public school teachers, nurses,
bus drivers, and postal workers. The black population on white college campuses is diversified. They have grown up in all sorts of
family structures and living arrangements. They come mainly from
working-class and middle-class families. Their general feeling of
financial uncertainty derives from the modest family income and their
dependency on nonfamily sources of support, which many black students
describe as untrustworthy. This feeling of uncertainty was found
again and again to serve as a distraction from their studies.

While the proportion of black students (57 percent) who talk about
their money worries with other students is not much different from
the proportion of white students (51 percent) who often carry on conversations about this topic, our interviews revealed some special
problems and frustrations. For example, black students said off-
campus jobs in the local community seemed to be less available to
them, compared with whites. This is supported by our survey data:
19 percent of the white students, compared with only 1.9 percent of
the black students, worked off campus as a way of partially financing
their education.

At the private colleges, money problems for black students were
particularly severe. Anne is a freshman student from a rural community. Her mother and father now teach in a foreign country. Her
remarks are typical.

The one thing I really found disillusioning about Cosmopolitan
College is the lack of financial output they have. When you are

TABLE 6

Sources of Financial Support for Black and White Students
at Four Upstate New York Colleges, 1969-70
(percent)

Sources of Support	Blacks (N=161)			Whites (N=200)		
	Male	Female	Total	Male	Female	Total
Scholarship	57.7	51.3	55.3	37.6	29.3	34.5
Work Off Campus	2.6	1.3	1.9	24.8	11.0	19.0
Spouse Works	1.3	0	.6	6.8	2.4	5.0
Parental Support	29.5	40.3	37.9	47.9	62.2	53.5
Work On Campus	9.0	11.3	9.9	11.1	9.8	10.5
Other	24.4	21.3	22.4	16.2	19.5	18.0

Note: The columns do not add up to 100 percent because some students indicated multiple sources of support.

81

on the outside and not in close quarters with the college, you
hear they have so much money. Guidance counselors tell
you that Cosmopolitan College has a lot of money to give for
financial aid. They don't give it to the black students. And
most of the black students don't need it. They're the ones
riding around in cars; and the girls have minks. Like, I
came up here with one coat.

By the time I finish school, if I go at the rate I'm going,
I'll have $12,000 [in] loans on my back at the end of four
years. I only have a $600 scholarship from the college.

They charge late fees for everything. My tuition was
late this time because my parents are [out of the country].
They charged me $25. Where was I supposed to get it from?
I don't know. The finances are just crippling. . . .

I started to work as soon as I got here at T_____ and
P_____ as a telephone solicitor. I lasted a week and a half.
I was working five nights a week, four hours a night, and I
just couldn't take it. Then I worked at the campus store.
That was all right but I still didn't like the idea of going to
school and working too. I stopped working at the campus
store at the beginning of this semester. All of my spending
money is gone. I just can't afford to keep going. I don't
know what is going to happen next year.

The way you hear about it, you think, "Oh great, I'll
apply and get some financial aid." And then you don't get
it. Every time you don't make [the] average [grade] . . .
they take away a hundred dollars of your scholarship or
something like that. . . . What's taking away $100 going to
do? All it's going to do is keep you away from coming here
next semester. You already put so much out; it's a waste
not to continue really like to get financial aid. I'd do all
right if I had that.

Several students commented about the scaling down of financial
aid during subsequent years of matriculation. "If a person was needy
when he got here, he should be much more needy after the [tuition]
raise," said Charles, a third-year student. He reasoned that one's
scholarship should go up instead of down. He states that after the
college enrolls a black student, scholastic aid is frequently cut, "which
was, after all, one of the basic things that got me here in the first
place." He asserts that his college is losing black students because

of this practice. Cynthia, a coed from a large family, also complains
about the administration of financial aid at Cosmopolitan College. "The
financial aid policy which makes it possible for the administration to
take back a scholarship at their discretion creates hardships, especially for black students." She goes on to say that "a large number
of black students could not stay at Cosmopolitan College without financial aid; as a result, if they lose their scholarships they usually
must leave school." Cynthia was particularly resentful of this financial
relationship between black students and the college administration,
which she characterizes as "dependency" for blacks. A final observation comes from Arthur, a sophomore psychology major, whose father
is a production helper in an upstate New York industrial community.
Arthur believes that the financial aid office looks upon black students
as potential financiers of their own education. "They don't seem to
realize that black students have grave financial problems. We don't
have mothers and fathers with high paying jobs and sometimes there
are a lot of children in the family." Most black students firmly believed that more blacks would go to college if there was more financial
aid available.

At this point, it should be reiterated that our study is from the
point of view of black students. The financial aid officers can field
most of these complaints with perfectly reasonable answers from their
point of view. The answers, however, may be inadequate from the
point of view of black students. Insecurity and uncertainty have been
their lot for so long that any attempt, legitimate or otherwise, to take
away any benefits they have been given is immediately interpreted as
a conspiracy to keep blacks down. Because of the racial inequality in
family income, demonstrated in this and other studies, blacks are
particularly edgy about financial manipulations. More than 70 percent
of the blacks attending these colleges say that they are there because
it is very important that they be able to look forward to a secure future.
Approximately 40 percent of the black students (compared with 14
percent of the white students) say it is very important that their college
education provide them with the opportunity to earn a great deal of
money. It is fair to say that a majority of white and black students
hope that a college education will contribute to their personal growth
and develop skills that will enable them to help others. However, the
deprived circumstances of most blacks cause the economic opportunities that college may open up to be much more significant to them than
they are to whites. Any reduction in college financial aid, therefore,
is a threat to the education and future security of young black people.

Blacks have much historical evidence that whites are not likely
to deal justly with them in money matters. College blacks have the

current reactions of their white classmates as evidence, too. Daily, they are confronted with attitudes such as those revealed in our study.

While 73 percent of the white students believed that the college should provide tutorial and other special help for black students if they were having problems in school work, only 40 percent believed that financial aid, such as special scholarships, should be reserved for blacks. Perhaps most whites oppose special opportunities for blacks because they believe there is no discrimination and, therefore, no need for preferential treatment. Indeed, 75 percent of the white students believed that there was equal access to scholarships and other financial aids at their schools.

The many complaints about financial aid indicate that some administrative officers at white colleges are insensitive to the severe economic deprivation of black people. These complaints also indicate that white colleges have not faced up to the financial dimensions of increasing the black student population. It is a responsibility of colleges and universities to provide a disproportionate amount of scholarship aid for disadvantaged students.

On the basis of our analysis, it would appear that white colleges are interested in recruiting more black students and that blacks attending these schools have similar interests. Black students tend to believe that they and the white colleges have different reasons for recruiting blacks but nevertheless are willing to cooperate because of the benefit they will derive from an enlarged black student body.

The coming together of black students and white college administrators around a common recruitment program, in which each presumably is participating for different reasons, is significant. It indicates that self-interest is an important component of social action and that it is possible to unite groups with disparate interests in a common cause if each group can fulfill its desires by completing the task jointly. It would appear that the fulfillment of self-interest is a stronger inducement for cooperative action than are altruistic motives.

8

To many blacks, a college education means a secure future. Of the black students in our study, 95 percent expressed this hope. Problems that could interrupt the college career or otherwise interfere with the security which an education might bring, as well as student aspirations, are analyzed in this chapter. By understanding both the problems and the possibilities of black students, impediments to their progress may be eliminated and their strengths reinforced.

Successful academic performance is probably one of the greatest challenges for blacks at white colleges. (See Tables 7 and 8.) Slightly less than one-fourth (23 percent) of all blacks, compared with nearly one-half (49 percent) of all whites, had accumulative grade-point averages of B and above. Moreover, the proportion of black students doing less than C work (14 percent) is four times greater than the proportion of white students (3.0 percent) who are performing poorly. (These are self-reported grade averages, which the students voluntarily recorded on our survey form—which was self-administered.) Of the black students at the white colleges in our study, 70 percent are in their first or second year. These tend to be the most difficult years in college, especially the first. Thus, an analysis of academic performance by year in school should be made before any hard and fast conclusions are drawn about the differential performance of black and white students.

Of all racial groups and class levels at the white colleges in our study, black freshmen experienced the greatest difficulty in academic performance. Only 14 percent of the first-year black students received average grades of B or above after their first semester of study at college, compared with 47 percent of the white freshmen. However, all black students did not perform at this low level:

TABLE 7

Self-Report Estimate of Cumulative Average of
Grades, by Year in School, for Black Students
at Four White Colleges in Upstate New York,
1969-70
(percent)

Average Grade	Graduate (N = 2)	Freshman (N =66)	Sopho-more (N=44)	Junior (N=26)	Senior (N=21)	Total (N=159)
A	—	3.0	—	3.8	4.8	2.5
B	—	10.6	22.7	19.2	47.6	20.1
C	100	63.7	63.7	73.2	47.6	63.6
D	—	22.7	13.7	3.8	—	13.8
F	—	—	—	—	—	—
Total	100	100.0	100.0	100.0	100.0	100.0

TABLE 8

Self-Report Estimate of Cumulative Average of
Grades, by Year in School, for White Students
at Four White Colleges in Upstate New York,
1969-70
(percent)

Average Grade	Graduate (N=23)	Freshman (N=71)	Sopho-more (N=49)	Junior (N=47)	Senior (N=14)	Total (N=204)
A	43.4	5.6	6.2	6.4	6.4	10.3
B	47.9	40.9	32.6	36.2	35.7	38.2
C	8.7	46.5	59.2	57.4	57.2	48.5
D	—	5.6	2.0	—	—	2.5
F	—	1.4	—	—	—	0.5
Total	100.0	100.0	100.0	100.0	100.0	100.0

second-year and third-year students, for example, jumped nearly ten
percentage points higher, with approximately ˜3 percent in each class
achieving A or B averages. While these students represented a notable
improvement in academic performance over their black freshmen
schoolmates, they nevertheless lagged behind the whites, of whom 39
percent of the second-year class and 43 percent of the third-year
class performed at levels that were evaluated as good to excellent.

By the fourth year, many black students had caught up with the
white students and were doing quite well. In fact, a majority (52 percent) of the black seniors had accumulative averages of A or B,
compared with 42 percent of the white seniors; as a collectivity, then,
the black fourth-year students in white colleges were performing
better than the white seniors in these schools. Thus, fourth-year
black students apparently have overcome many of the impediments
that tend to interfere with academic excellence during the first three
years of college.

Intensive analysis of fourth-year black students should be undertaken to determine why and how they have survived. An understanding
of how the black seniors persevered and transcended the difficulties
of academic work would be helpful to other blacks as well as to whites,
who, as we saw, lag behind their black schoolmates at the senior
level. It is particularly important that an intensive analysis be done
of fourth-year black students, compared with first-, second-, and third-
year blacks. Several factors in addition to academic preparation may
be involved. Of all blacks at the four colleges in our study, 61 percent,
compared with 70 percent of the whites, classified themselves as above-
average achievers in high school. Only 4 percent of the blacks and
3 percent of the whites said that they were below average. The large
difference in black and white performance during the freshman year
is much greater than expected in the light of this modest difference
by race in self-reported high school achievement.

The outstanding performance of black seniors is indicative of
the motivation and drive that characterizes many black students at
white colleges. Though the grade-point average of blacks during
their first three years of college lags behind that of whites, our study
reveals that blacks are no less ambitious than whites about continuing
their education beyond the bachelor's degree. About seven out of
every ten of the black and white students say that they plan to pursue
graduate studies, and nearly one-fourth (24 percent of the blacks
and 23 percent of the whites) want a doctorate degree.

TABLE 9

Evaluations by Black and White Students at Four White Colleges in Upstate New York of Educational Opportunities in Graduate Schools Today, Compared with Five Years Ago, 1964-65 and 1969-70
(percent)

Graduate School	Black Evaluation				White Evaluation			
	As Good or Better	Not As Good	Not Sure	Total	As Good or Better	Not As Good	Not Sure	Total
Professional:								
Law	58.9	30.7	10.4	100.0	66.2	22.4	11.4	100.0
Medicine	61.1	30.9	8.0	100.0	71.2	18.4	10.4	100.0
Engineering	58.0	28.4	13.6	100.0	71.1	19.4	9.5	100.0
Discipline:								
Sciences	51.5	35.6	12.9	100.0	71.7	16.4	11.9	100.0
Social Sciences	74.9	15.3	9.8	100.0	81.6	10.9	7.5	100.0

Blacks want to go to graduate school but question whether or not they will be accepted. We asked the students in our survey if they thought black college graduates with good grades had as good a chance as white students with the same grades of getting into a top school. A majority of all of the black students believed that the opportunity to get into a good graduate school is as good or better today for blacks than five years ago, as seen in Table 9. Of the black students, 75 percent felt that opportunities to study in the social sciences were open to them and that they had as good a chance or even a better chance, compared with five years ago, of being accepted today in a top school in these field. For the other four areas listed in our survey, including the sciences, engineering, law, and medicine, the proportion of blacks who thought they had a good or better chance of being accepted in a good school if their grades were good varied from 52 to 61 percent.

The average response of all blacks for the five graduate program areas combined was a favorable 61 percent, indicating they believe the educational opportunity system was opening up to accommodate them. While this finding may be comforting to some, in that it represents the feelings of a majority of black college students, it also is disquieting, in that it points out that approximately 40 percent are either uncertain or believe that there has been no progress and that things are even getting worse. Thus, one may conclude that among black students on white college campuses, a lack of consensus exists concerning opportunities at the graduate level. There is evidence that a majority of blacks believe that they will be able to experience continuity in their studies, unhampered by racial discrimination in admission to graduate school; yet a very large minority have their doubts or assess the situation differently.

The doubt and disbelief about fair treatment on the part of graduate schools are similarly held by all black students, no matter what year in school they may be. Combining all five graduate areas, an average of 38 percent of the black senior class doubt or disbelieve that graduate schools will accept black people on their merit. The figure is similar to the 40 percent average obtained for freshmen who have similar feelings. The apologists for the system might be tempted to explain the feelings of first-year students regarding the fairness of admissions procedures for graduate school as a rationalization of their poor academic performance. But no such explanation can be attached to the feelings of fourth-year black students, who, as a group, performed academically better than whites. The black seniors are, and know that they are, capable of doing graduate work. Their disbelief and doubt are probably due to the racism that persists in this nation and to the racial inequality that is institutionalized.

We also examined the postcollege work plans of black students at white colleges. The categories were predetermined on the survey form, so the findings presented here do not represent the range of occupational choices of black students. They do indicate, however, how black students feel about some of the major employment areas in our society.

Of the black students at the colleges included in our study, 75 to 85 percent said that opportunities for employment in teaching and social work were as good or better today than they were five years ago, as seen in Table 10. These, of course, are professions that traditionally have been more open to blacks. Doubt sets in as the conversation shifts to a discussion of opportunities in industry, commerce, and government. The proportion of black students who believe that the employment opportunities in these areas are equal to, or better than, those that existed a few years ago ranges from 55 percent down to 45 percent. It is surprising to note that the institutional system (among the five listed) that blacks felt was doing the least in 1969-70, when this survey was conducted, was the government. A majority of the black students either were not sure or said employment opportunities in the government were not as good in 1969-70 as they had been five years earlier. Thus, we see almost a fifty-to-fifty division between blacks who believe, on the one hand, that chances for employment are better and those, on the other hand, who are uncertain or who believe that chances for a black person are worse today. Therefore, we are faced with a situation of increasing certainty by blacks that they will get a college education (due in part to the attempts by white schools to redress the racial unbalance of their student bodies) but uncertainty that they will get a good job. And so the frustration continues.

The hopes and aspirations of blacks do not occur within a vacuum. Whether or not they are fulfilled depends in part upon the reactions of whites to their protests and challenges. Herein lies a dilemma. Whites often refuse to act decisively to redress the grievances of blacks because they believe that they have already acted and that the good times have already arrived for all. Tables 9 and 10 indicate that the white students believed in all instances that opportunities for employment and graduate education were more open to blacks than blacks indicated they were. The conjectures of white students about the openness of the employment and educational opportunity systems in America, on the average, were consistently ten percentage points higher than the estimates by blacks. For example, 65 percent of the white students, compared to 55 percent of the black students, said that employment opportunities in industry were better today

TABLE 10

Evaluations by Black and White Students at Four White Colleges in Upstate
New York of Employment Opportunities for Blacks Today,
Compared with Five Years Ago, 1964-65 and 1969-70
(percent)

	Black Evaluation				White Evaluation			
Job	As Good or Better	Not As Good	Not Sure	Total	As Good or Better	Not as Good	Not Sure	Total
Government	44.8	48.5	6.7	100.0	59.2	34.8	5.0	100.0
Industry	54.7	38.5	6.8	100.0	65.0	28.0	7.0	100.0
Retail Business	47.8	39.9	12.3	100.0	53.7	36.3	10.0	100.0
Teaching	76.1	17.8	6.1	100.0	85.1	10.9	4.0	100.0
Social Work	83.4	12.3	4.3	100.0	89.6	5.0	5.4	100.0

for blacks. Likewise, 71 percent of the white students, compared to
61 percent of the black students, said that chances were as good or
better today that a black person would be accepted for medical school.

The rosier picture of the status of race relations that white
students have painted for themselves is probably a psychological
mechanism of denial. It tends to desensitize them to the real agony
and pain experienced by black students at white colleges. Such desen-
sitized people are not likely to entertain more demands, hear new
grievances, or respond with affirmative action when they honestly
believe that the problem is almost solved. These distorted perceptions
by whites interfere with the full participation of blacks in educational
and employment opportunities in this society and, therefore, place in
jeopardy the possibility of a future that is secure.

9

BLACK STUDENTS
AND THE
LOCAL
COMMUNITY

Since the establishment of residential colleges in the United States, the relationship between college students and the communities in which these colleges are located has been an important concern. Though the town-gown relationship has traditionally referred to the social interaction between students and the community, it has in recent years broadened to include the students' involvement in local electoral processes and in community organizations. The growing number of black students on predominantly white college campuses has added a new dimension to these two aspects of college-community relations.

Intensive recruitment programs by white colleges have brought black students to areas where traditionally there have been few. This situation often is a new experience for the black student, as well as for the local community. Two of the colleges studied, Small City College and Little Village College, are located in rural areas. The absence of blacks in the surrounding areas is one of the major complaints of black students attending these colleges. We found that the presence of other blacks is needed by campus blacks for their indirect benefit, in that public facilities for the accomodation of community blacks also may be used by students. A black student at Cosmopolitan College in Metropolitan City, which has a black population of several thousand persons, speaks with delight about his retreat from the white campus from time to time to rap with blacks in a local barber shop. Another student at the same school says that about 95 percent of his activities are centered on campus but that he does patronize the black bars in the community.

While some students find the local facilities in Metropolitan City satisfactory, others, especially students who come from larger

urban areas, say there is nothing to do. One student from New York
City called Metropolitan City "a bunch of crap." His reference was
to the lack of places to go. Another student talked about the limited
opportunity to see black artists perform in the theatre in a community
like Metropolitan City, compared with New York City. While the
modest facilities available for the accommodation of the black community in this middle-sized city are tabbed as insufficient and inadequate by some, the black students at white colleges in small communities where no black families reside are very much dissatisfied.

One black student estimated that approximately three-fourths of
the blacks at Little Village College go home on the weekend" for
socializing purposes" because there is nothing to do in Little Village;
there are no black bars or black night clubs. "Nothing to do," "now-
where to go"—these are sentiments expressed by many black students.
Some students attributed the absence of adequate facilities to the fact
that the town is small, while others specifically indicated the absence
of a black community as the reason why no satisfactory facilities
are available. Thus, on weekends, black students on these campuses
go home, go to Metropolitan City, or go to other nearby urban areas
for recreation. Black students at white colleges in small towns who
do not have access to transportation for weekend trips away from
the campus feel as if they were trapped, imprisoned, and isolated.
Melvin, a senior political science major at Small City College,
summed up the situation this way, "No matter where you go, you are
going to be surrounded by whites."

Small City and Little Village are not without some recreational
facilities. Each community has a few bars, restaurants, bowling
alleys, and theatres. However, racial prejudice, real or imagined,
presents a barrier to their free use by black students. Moreover,
some black students say that they are uncomfortable in places of
public accommodation that are patronized predominantly by whites.
Irene, a second-year student, tells about her off-campus excursion
in Little Village a year earlier, when only fifteen black students
were enrolled at her college. "I went downtown one day by myself.
I went into a store and the lady just looked at me and stood there.
Then her husband came out from the back [of the store]. He said
he'd help me look for something and he did. [They] may have not
met blacks before. . . ." Melvin had a similar experience when he
went to church in Small City. "By me being the only black [present],"
he said, "the people acted as if I had stepped off a spaceship and I
was something unusual. The looks and the feelings I got from the
people!" Irene surmises that many of the students and townspeople
in Little Village have grown up without seeing any blacks. She

believes this to be their basic reason for finding it "hard" to accept
blacks. Melvin has a stronger view; he called the whites hypocritical
because "they can't accept people." Two male students complained
about the white bars in Little Village, and one said this is why the
blacks tend to drink in their rooms. In a defiant mood, possibly trying
to blot out his feelings of isolation and loneliness, Mark said: "Why
should I go downtown and drink beer and come back? I can buy a
six-pack and drink it right here in my room. Why should I spend my
money with them? It's cheaper this way."

        Other black students indicate that more than discomfort keeps
them away from the white places of public accommodation. "It's
bad to go into town at night for a drink," said George, a freshman at
Small City College. "They're always making remarks against the
blacks and the long-haired hippies." Amos, another student at the
same college, told a story about a fight that his friend Lester almost
got into in a restaurant and store in Small City; it happened during
the summer months when not many students were on campus. "[Lester]
and his buddies went over to this restaurant. There were all Italians
in the store and one them called [Lester] 'nigger.' Lester thought of
fighting but then [thought again]: 'Why do it? We don't want to be there
with them so bad as to fight with them.'" Amos also knows that blacks
who have tried to get housing off campus in Small City have been dis-
criminated against. For him, Small City "is not right for any black
man!"

        Despite negative feelings about the local white community,
blacks have joined white students in calling for relevancy in the college
curriculum, which would include more involvement with the community
surrounding the campus. On one of our campuses, this call has
resulted in the establishment of a college-credit Community Intern-
ship Program to serve as a means for the students to get involved
in the community in many different ways. We found that prior to
this new program, few students, black or white, were deeply involved in local community affairs. During the study year, only 25
percent of the students had volunteered or worked for a community
social welfare agency that year. At the other three schools, the
figures were even smaller: 20 percent or less for whites and 16
percent for blacks. It remains to be seen whether or not this recently developed effort to increase involvement of students with the
local community will modify this minimum amount of participation.

        Throughout our interviews, the black students expressed desires
to go back to their black communities after college, to work with
and for their people rather than to seek only individual success.

Some students in the two colleges in Metropolitan City, where there
is a local black population, are not waiting for graduation. In addition to their studies, they are working individually and through
programs of the black student organizations to get involved in the
local black community. However, in general, the actual participation
of black students in the daily affairs of the local black community is
little and limited.

The proportion of black students who have moderate to strong
beliefs that college should prepare students to be community leaders
varies from a high of 52 percent at Little Village College to a low of
26 percent at Small City College. The other two, Cosmopolitan
College and Metropolitan College, are in-between, with 43 and 33
percent of their black students, respectively, who have similar beliefs.
In general, however, black students, while in college, do not seek
experience for this role by getting involved with the local black community. A discrepancy between belief and action is illustrated at
Little Village College. Only about 17 percent of the black students
had participated and/or given leadership in marches, demonstrations,
or other protest movements off campus during the school year, although three times as many believed themselves to be in training for
positions of black leadership. Militant protest, of course, is not
the only kind of community leadership that students could provide.
However, we thought that this avenue of service should be checked
out, since only 25 percent or less engage in more moderate activity,
like volunteer service in local health, welfare, and recreation programs. Thus, the proportion of black student activists involved in
all kinds of off-campus activities is consistently less than 50 percent.
There exists a discrepancy between black students' statements about
their need to become involved with community people at the grass
roots level and their actual behavior. Black students call for an
education that is relevant, but their limited participation in the community indicates that they are not oriented to learning by doing.

A common complaint among 66 percent or more of the black
students at all colleges is that they do not have an opportunity to
meet people who live in the community surrounding their schools.
In places like Little Village and Small City, students tend to attribute
this difficulty to the lack of blacks in the local community. Even in
a community like the middle-sized Metropolitan City, where there
are 15, 000 to 20, 000 blacks, 90 percent of the black students at
Cosmopolitan College say there is little opportunity to meet local
community people, which would include the black population. Thus,
the barriers against frequent interaction between campus and community blacks appears to be something more than the availability of
a local black community.

Part of the strained relation may be due to the attitudes of college blacks toward local blacks. In Metropolitan City, for example, where there are many blacks, who exhibit varying styles of life, we found that the students tended to stereotype them. After spending three years in this community, Caroline, who came from a middle-class southern family, in which her father is a physician and her mother, a teacher, said: "Most of the people I know in [Metropolitan City] are very suppressed. . . . The people are very complacent and apathetic. They've been here so long, they don't want to do anything about it and the situation becomes stagnant. It seems to me most of the [black] people are uneducated." Another black student, Olivia, who had participated in a tutoring program in one of the Metropolitan City elementary schools near the campus, on the edge of a black ghetto, said:

> I got a general impression of the black community. I learned through [the children's] descriptions of their home life, how life was for most blacks in [Metropolitan City]. I got a depressing view because . . . I guess, coming from New York where blacks are quite pushy in comparison to blacks here who are so downtrodden . . . [The blacks here] just sort of exist.

Evelyn, a sophomore at the same college, expressed the belief that local community blacks feel that black students "look down" on them. The testimonies of her campus colleagues, Caroline and Olivia, would seem to offer sufficient reasons for blacks in the community to feel this way. Catherine summed up the town-gown situation this way:

> We don't really have . . . close contact with the black people in the city, partially because some of the blacks [on campus] have the idea that we are the students and they are the townies, [and] also because a lot of people in the city have hostile attitudes toward the black people who go [to Cosmopolitan College]. They see the college as an oppressive institution; we are part of that institution. We're obviously not lacking for money, since we have the funds to go [to college] here. And there are always the [students] who want to go down into the community to help 'the poor un-fortunates' and that attitude shows. A lot of people are changing their attitudes about people in the com-munity but I'd say the great majority of the black kids who go here are really out of touch with the black com-munity. They're middle class. . . .

Catherine's remarks indicate that social class may account for the
separation between campus and community blacks. Thus, the unity
that black students profess to seek with other blacks seems to be
unity among blacks with similar education.

An example of this separation is the founding of a black church
on one of the campuses. The black church, a nondemoninational
organization set up by the Union of Black Collegians, began as a
campus activity. The minister is a student who has already completed
theological seminary training. The church features a gospel choir
of talented students, which has appeared on local television. The
First Black International Church (a fictitious name to protect the
anonymity of the campus) was characterized by Glasco, a freshman,
as a "revolutionary church," aimed at liberating all oppressed people.
"[It] will include all different religions and will try to deal with high
school students also," he said. Geneva, a sophomore from the Middle
West, whose father is a clergyman, sees the First Black International
Church as a missionary instrument, through which campus blacks may
penetrate the local black community. Geneva said:

> I don't know very much about the [black community in
> this area]. However, I am now getting ready to get
> very much involved with it with the black church. We
> are going to move the church into the community
> sometime in the near future. We are going to start
> going for Sunday School. I feel that one of the best
> ways to get into the black community [in this area]
> is to start working with the children, because, I
> think, it is easier to reach the children. . . . The
> adults aren't too receptive towards anybody who goes
> to [this college]. If you could reach the children and
> show them that black students are not [like the rest of
> the people at this college], the parents will eventually
> come around. Then there won't be as much static
> between black students and the black community.

Instead of encouraging students to fan out from the campus community
to participate in the existing and established black religious con-
gregations as a means of becoming involved with, and helping, local
blacks, the students organized their own church, so that their own
ideas of what a church should be might prevail.

A theme that emerged from our interviews with the students is
that local blacks dislike campus blacks because of their disdain for
the college as a community institution and the oppressive power that
it allegedly exercises. Said Rosalind, a junior from New York City:

> As the [college] expands, it displaces [black] people [in
> the surrounding community] without any regard for them.
> The resulting college-community conflict affects the
> black students. The black people from the community
> relate their disdain for the college to the black student
> as a part of it. This causes disunity among black
> students and towners where there should be unity.

No information was obtained from local community blacks to
determine the truth or falsity of this explanation. By attributing the
perceived animosity between local and campus blacks to institutional
expansion policies of the students' college, the campus blacks may
be rationalizing an uncomfortable situation of racial disunity.

Black college students seem to see their thrusts into the surrounding black community as being for the benefit of those whom the
students have classified as "less fortunate." However, they do not
appear to recognize that these thrusts are usually on their terms.
Their activities in the local community tend to violate the principle
of self-determination for local blacks. The black students affirm and
jealously guard this principle in their interactions with whites on
campus but tend to forget it when working with the local black community. They approached local community blacks very much in the
tradition of Rudyard Kipling, as if they were "the black student's
burden." Despite their limited knowledge and involvement with the
local community, black students are actively designing programs,
such as the First Black International Church and its Sunday School,
for other blacks, but are not inviting them to participate in the program-
design process. This is contrary to the principle of self-determination.

At Metropolitan College, a two-year school that caters to local
residents, we found a similar attitude among black students with respect to planning for the black community. In a discussion group,
these remarks were made:

> [We're], like, on an added pedestal because [we're]
> black and [we're] in college. [We need a] community
> relations program [at this school] that tells you about
> organizing in the community. [We need to learn how]
> to do it the way the organizers have done it before,
> and on things that relate to the community. How can
> we best benefit our community? Maybe if we had a
> black instructor who dealt specifically with this, maybe
> he could help us obtain these goals. We could bring
> the black community of [Metropolitan City] up to par or

to surpass the white community or, at least, to work on
an even keel with them.

The topic of the black student's responsibility for his community
was a recurring theme. "We don't want to forget where we came
from," said a black woman student. Another chimed in:

> We want to go back and help them and make them come
> up too—help them, and do anything in our power to do
> that. And too, when we can get this instilled in their
> minds, [we can] make them see that what we're doing
> for them [is] a sacrifice. We're not doing it because
> we're getting paid or something like that. It's
> voluntary because we want the black community to
> rise. We want to see black people assume their
> place, their rightful place in society. Not until that
> time can we be of any good. So going into different
> programs is good. But we have to go into them with
> sincerity, with the attitude that we're doing it for the
> black people and make the black people No. 1 on [our]
> list, make the black community part of [us], part of
> the individual. And when we can do that, then we're
> over. I think the [Student Afro-American Society] has
> got what it takes because we have a strong nucleus.
> We have enough workers there to do it. Yes, we could
> really be persuasive. If we'd just get ourselves to-
> gether, get off our asses and do something. That's all
> we really need to do.

There is little recognition by students that black adults, including the
unlettered and the inarticulate, might have something to say to the
young.

In summary, racial discrimination for black students is a
persisting problem, especially in villages and in towns with no black
population and tends to interfere with their free use of local facilities
and places of public accommodation. Black students benefit from an
enlarged local black population. At colleges located in areas with
a local black community, the black students tend to feel more comfortable patronizing the community facilities that have been established to service the personal, recreational, and other leisure time
needs of the local blacks. Moreover, in communities with relatively
large black populations, local whites are less inclined to stare and
gaze at black college students as odd and uncommon sights. However,
in these communities, direct interaction between campus and

community blacks and the identification of students with the local black community is limited. Disunity between campus and community blacks is probably due not so much to ideology and different goals as to variations in education and to different, and sometimes incompatible, life-styles. The principle of self-determination, which black students affirm in their relationships with whites on the college campus, tends to be forgotten in their associations with blacks in the local community. Students tend to design programs for the black community without the participation of other blacks in the program-design process.

10

Despite the recent hullabaloo and the widely announced recruitment programs, black students at white colleges are still rare. There were only 384 black students on the campuses of the four colleges included in this study. This represents less than 2 percent of the combined student bodies of 26,750. Even when the expensive private college is excluded from the total and only public institutions are considered, black students on these campuses still are only 1.6 percent of all students. Yet the presence of black students on white college campuses is shaking the foundations of these institutions. Seldom have so few stimulated concern and consternation that could affect so many and which could lead to fundamental changes in the structure of the college campus. Indeed, it is good that white colleges are taking cognizance of themselves in response to the challenges of blacks. Institutions that stand firm and refuse to even consider new methods and directions in education may soon fall, like Goliath before David.

The tangle of pathology in race relations in America is revealed on the college campus in full-dress confusion and circumlocution. Many whites reject blacks and many blacks reject whites, and both groups claim that their actions are without malice. Both blacks and whites sometimes even assert that segregation or separatism is for the protection of the rejected race.

Our data lead us to believe that the separatist movement of black students on many college campuses is not merely a fad or something that will soon pass. With more interaction between the races on campus as the number of black students increases, the level of trust between blacks and whites appears to decrease. This may be due to an unmasking effect, which the increased interaction has produced. We have discovered that most blacks came to white colleges expecting to find less prejudice, less discrimination, and more social integration than they actually encounter. Their confidence and trust in whites has been shaken by cruel, or, at the very least, thoughtless, insults and insensitivity. For many blacks, these experiences have been a cause for anger and despair, have contributed to their call for separation and withdrawal, and have encouraged some to seek reparation and revenge. Their actions have also been supported by forces for change in the relationship between blacks and whites in the larger society.

Due to this general lack of trust, many black students believe that they may turn only to other black students for social life. On a psychological level, it is a well-documented fact that every individual needs social support and validation of his self-concept in order to function effectively.

A considerable amount of separation, black from white, already has taken place in living arrangements. Of the black students, 75 percent have lived with black roommates most of their college career or now have black roommates. An increasing number have expressed preference not only for black roommates but also for all-black sections within dormitories. The all-black dormitory, though much discussed, is not a preferred housing arrangement for most black students so far. If the new anti-integration living arrangements that are emerging—the racially homogeneous roommate system and the racially homogeneous dormitory section—are viewed as progressive responses to the presence of racism and if the experience of racism does not abate for black students on white college campuses, then the all-black dormitory could quickly become a preferred housing arrangement for a majority of the blacks, and an increasingly impenetrable boundary would be built up between black and white students.

In our opinion, the extreme form of social separation—the all-black dormitory—could be both beneficial and harmful to black students. Such isolation could protect black students from the subtle and blatant racist insults that they continually experience in dormitories. But, an isolated, easily identifiable housing facility, separated from the rest of the campus because of racist attitudes and mistrust, could in turn become a target for much racist-motivated mischief. In this respect, the all-black dormitory could be harmful to blacks. The number of blacks who prefer a racially homogeneous black dormitory is slightly more than one-fourth, but, as one student estimated, only about one-fifth would choose to live in such a housing facility. This proportion is the same as that of blacks who have lived only with whites on campus. Thus, a majority, or three-fifths, of the black students prefer some kind of living arrangement neither exclusively black nor exclusively white.

On campuses where the number of blacks is less than seventy-five, the black students have suffered the social consequences of an inadequate range of personalities and social types with whom to develop compatible relations. This situation tends to increase anxiety. (Because of last-chance or once-in-a-lifetime fears, which often characterizes dating, one partner may press prematurely for an exclusive relationship.) Due to their fear of being trapped and not knowing how to gracefully handle a premature move for exclusivity, the black males and females on the campus communities where the number of black students is small often hang loose in their relationship with each other, exhibiting standoffish and indifferent attitudes. On those campuses where black-white interaction is estranged and the opportunities for blacks to interact with other blacks are few, feelings such as those mentioned above further complicate the situation and limit social life.

Moreover, because of their common experience of racial segregation, many blacks who are forced upon each other for social life tend to begin their relationships with each other on a brother-sister basis. They tend to take each other for granted rather than cultivate relationships. Interaction becomes so intense that most relationships are treated as primary relationships, even those that would probably have remained impersonal and secondary in other circumstances. This means that many blacks on white college campuses act as if they have almost unlimited access to all other blacks—the brothers and sisters—such as might occur in a family. The kinship system is particularly the model for relationships between blacks on white college campuses where their numbers are small. For some, this kind of social arrangement is comfortable and generates considerable security; for others, it is confining and oppressive. Certainly, freedom of association and flexibility in movement are limited and impaired in a black campus community that takes on the characteristics of an extended family.

That more blacks are being recruited in white colleges and that a number of white students want blacks on campus and want them to live in their midst in the dormitories should not be interpreted as a sign that black and white students are beginning to make common cause. Whites still have limited interest in racial problems on campus or in the community. Less than 10 percent discuss such issues frequently. With blacks, discussion of the racial situation is a consuming experience. Several colleges have increased the number of blacks in their student body but have not recognized that blacks and whites have some interests and concerns that are essentially different. The attempt to treat black students as if they were white students ignores the contemporary and historical oppression that blacks have experienced. Racial discrimination is the fundamental difference in the black and white experience in America. Neither this difference nor its consequences can or should be denied.

One consequence of racial discrimination is the lack of trust between blacks and whites. Black students on white college campuses feel the need for someone in authority whom they can trust and to whom they can turn for advice about ways of negotiating the college system. Because they currently perceive the white campus community as hostile, that person with whom they may consult should not be white. Thus, a new and as yet ambiguous role has emerged. It is the role of the black advisor.

Black students expect the black advisor to be an intercessor, to negotiate with the administration and faculty on their behalf. The advisor also is expected to be a resource to the black students, keeping them informed about campus happenings. The basic function of the black advisor is to provide support for the black students.

The black advisor performs a sort of holding operation, supporting the black students until the institution can demonstrate to them that it is trustworthy and reliable. Without a black advisor, the black students would despair. Their despair could turn into fury. Our data indicate that the age or sex of the advisor is unimportant, so long as the advisor gives authentic support to the students.

The black advisor is particularly important because black students at white colleges tend to distrust the faculty. Among the complaints by black students is that white teachers ignore, disregard, or avoid them. A more frequent complaint is that white teachers do not comprehend, or refuse to relate to, the black experience. The black advisor can provide essential links of trust between black students and white faculty. Estrangement between black students and white teachers is so great that black students tend to register complaints more often with the administration than directly with the teacher.

Black students felt that existing course materials were inadequate because they ignored the black experience and were oriented toward the educational needs of whites. Moreover, they felt that course materials would be useless after graduation, in that they would not equip them to work with, and help, other people, a main goal of their education.

Black students indicated they would like a Black Studies Program to serve various purposes: a way to learn essential information, to understand the history of one's people, to promote black identity and solidarity, to provide relevant academic experiences, to "straighten oneself out," and to chart goals for the future.

Most black students agree that the program of Black Studies should be controlled by blacks. Not all black students agree on whether whites should be allowed to take Black Studies courses or to teach them. Some black students see these courses as a way of teaching whites about blacks, but more want Black Studies to help blacks learn about themselves. Almost all blacks felt that only black professors should teach these courses, but a few said that when qualified black people are not available, extra, extra-qualified whites would be acceptable.

Black Studies is a program that fulfills many purposes, all of which must be considered when assessing its value. It is a bona fide academic program dealing with a valid intellectual concern. It is a political instrument through which power relationships are balanced between blacks and whites in the academic community. It is a means for initial employment for black professors at white institutions. It is a manifestation of the movement for black self-determination.

Although black students are deeply suspicious of the motives of teachers and administrators at white schools, they will participate in recruiting more blacks. In fact, black students encourage other blacks to go to white colleges, even though they are dissatisfied with the way blacks are treated, because more political power, a more adequate social life, and a better educational experience are products of a larger black student population.

Black students believe that white colleges still have quotas. Also, they believe that public colleges recruit blacks only because they are required to participate in specially funded programs for disadvantaged minorities. In general, they believe that white colleges that recruit black students are more interested in improving their institutional images than in helping black individuals.

An increasing number of black students receive financial aid from white schools, but deeply distrust these institutions. Any reduction in financial aid is threatening to black students because their family resources are limited. Many blacks said that they would have to leave college if their financial aid were lowered or cut. This financial uncertainty is often a distraction from their studies.

A liberal financial aid program must underlie any special recruitment program of blacks. However, most white colleges have
not faced up to the financial dimensions of an enlarged black student
population, which should require the reservation of a disproportionate
amount of scholarship resources for blacks and other minorities.

Many blacks tend to look upon a college education as a means to
a secure future. However, blacks who go to college encounter all
kinds of difficulties, academic and otherwise. While black freshmen
tend to perform less well than whites, black seniors tend to do better.
More information is needed to determine how black college seniors
have succeeded.

Despite their successful performance, many fourth-year black
students, along with their other black schoolmates, doubt that they
will be able to get a good job. A majority believe that chances are
better today than they were a few years ago, but a large minority are
uncertain. Whether or not the hopes and aspirations of blacks are
fulfilled depends in part upon the responses of whites. Whites are
increasingly less willing to redress the grievances of blacks, because
they tend to believe that the racial situation is better than blacks say
it is.

Black students at colleges in traditionally all-white communities
experience racial prejudice and discrimination on and off campus.
The existence of a local black community tends to cushion the effects
of this. It provides personal services and recreational facilities the
black students can utilize. However, cooperative interaction between
black students and local blacks on the solution of community problems
is limited. When it does occur, it is often patronizing and on the
terms of the students, who fail to follow through on their beliefs of
self-determination, which they jealously guard when interacting with
whites but tend to forget in their relations with other blacks.

The following are statements of the policy implications of our
study of the social and academic life of black students on white college
campuses.

1. The black advisor is a necessity on any white college campus.
Blacks should be retained to perform administrative, instructional,
and counseling functions. Since these functions may be conflicting,
one black staff member should not be expected to fulfill all of them.
White college administrators should guard against asking the advisor
or counselor to represent the school's interest in relating to black
students. The presence of black staff is important as a way of cement-
ing trust between black students and white institutions.

2. <u>Any white college deliberately recruiting black students
should enroll a large enough number to ensure an adequate social life
and educational experience</u>. There should be enough black students
present to provide a range of potentially compatible personalities and
social types. Also, the number should be sufficiently large so that
all need not be known to each other personally. The goal is to have
enough black students to provide freedom in association, flexibility
in movement, and anonymity when desirable.

3. <u>A disproportionate amount of financial aid should be reserved
for disadvantaged students</u>. White colleges must face this fact and
recognize that past economic deprivations of black and brown people
require extraordinary effort on the part of white institutions.

4. <u>Black Studies is a bona fide academic program and deals
with a valid intellectual concern</u>. It fulfills educational, economic,
and political goals for black students, all of which must be considered
when establishing a program.

5. <u>A diversity of housing opportunities are required for black
students at white colleges</u>, ranging all the way from opportunities to
live only with whites to opportunities to live only with blacks. Blacks
living with blacks appears to be the preferred living arrangement for
a majority of black students on white college campuses, but not necessarily in a separate black dormitory.

6. <u>The basic black-white issue on the white college campus is
not black separatism but white racism</u>, though both may constitute a
dilemma for people in charge. We feel that black separatism should
be neither endorsed nor opposed, but immediate steps should be taken
to end white racism. The hypothesis on which this recommendation
is based is this: eradication of expressions of white racism should
eliminate preferences for black separatism.

America is not without extensive experience, both good and bad,
in attempting to educate black people. The first major attempt was
made after the Civil War. In describing the earliest attempts,
W. E. B. DuBois informs us that "the opposition to Negro education
in the South was at first bitter, and showed itself in ashes, insult,
and blood; for the South believed an educated Negro to be a dangerous
Negro."[1] Nevertheless, schools like Morehouse, Fisk, Atlanta, How-
ard, and Hampton were founded during this period with public and
private assistance, like that rendered by the Freedmen's Bureau and
national religious groups. Although these schools were founded by
people with broad ideas and a self-sacrificing spirit, DuBois said that
some schools, which he chose not to mention by name, "were . . .

[deserving] of ridicule."[2] They did the best that they could with what they had but that often was not enough.

Despite the slow motion, the picture is clearly changing, 100 years after the emancipation of the black slaves in America. During a recent four-year period, 1964-68, the proportion of blacks in college increased from 8 to 15 percent.[3] The predominantly black colleges now enroll only about a half of the black students in higher education.[4] A new pattern in the place where black people are educated is emerging, and it involves the North as well as the South. It remains to be seen whether this new development in Negro education will also be met with "ashes, insult, and blood." Already, the confrontations on some college campuses indicate these are real possibilities.

NOTES

1. W. E. Burghardt DuBois, The Souls of Black Folk (Greenwich, Conn.: Fawcett, 1961) (first published in 1903), p. 36.

2. Ibid., p. 44.

3. Current Population Reports, U.S. Bureau of the Census (Series P-20 No. 190, School Enrollment, October 1967 and 1968) (Washington, D.C.: U. S. Government Printing Office, 1969), quoted in Warren W. Willingham, Admission of Minority Students in Midwestern Colleges (Evanston, Ill.: College Entrance Examination Board, Report M-1, 1970), p. 2.

4. Earl J. McGrath, The Predominantly Negro College and University in Transition (New York: Teachers College, Columbia University, 1965).

CHARLES V. WILLIE is Vice President for Student Affairs at Syracuse University where he has served as a faculty member since 1952. He is also Professor of Sociology and a former Chairman of the Department of Sociology. His areas of specialization are the sociology of education, social problems, health, and community organization. He has been a Visiting Lecturer in Sociology at the Harvard Medical School. From 1962 to 1964 he was Research Director of the Washington, D. C. Project of the President's Committee on Juvenile Delinquency and Youth Crime.

Born in Dallas, Texas, Professor Willie has lived in southern and northern regions of the United States and has attended predominantly black and predominantly white colleges and universities. His B. A. degree was earned at Morehouse College in Atlanta, Georgia, and his Ph. D. degree at Syracuse University.

A member of the Board of Directors of the Social Science Research Council, Professor Willie is a fellow of the American Sociological Association and a member of the American Public Health Association. He has written several articles on race-related topics and is editor of The Family Life of Black People and Racism and Mental Health.

ARLINE SAKUMA McCORD is currently an Assistant Professor at Hunter College, City University of New York. She received her undergraduate education and her doctorate in sociology at the University of Washington, Seattle. Previously, Dr. McCord taught in the California State College System and at Syracuse University. Her primary interests lie in the fields of social psychology, ethnic relations, formal organization, and the study of creativity. In addition to various articles on social psychology, she is co-author of a forthcoming book, Educational Opportunity and the Ghetto Child. She is, at the moment, completing a study on human strife and conflict.